IRONHORSE

A HISTORY OF THE STEAM TRAIN

IRONHORSE

A HISTORY OF THE STEAM TRAIN

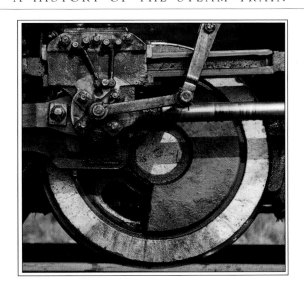

Peter Lorie & Colin Garratt

CRESCENT BOOKS

New York • Avenel

IRONHORSE

A LABYRINTH BOOK

IRON HORSE – A HISTORY OF THE STEAM TRAIN

© Labyrinth Publishing S.A. 1987
This edition copyright © 1996 by Labyrinth Publishing (UK) Ltd.

This 1996 edition is published by Crescent Books,
a division of Random House Value Publishing, Inc.,
40 Engelhard Avenue, Avenel, New Jersey 07001

Crescent Books and colophon are registered trademarks of
Random House Value Publishing Inc.

Random House
New York • Toronto • London • Sydney • Auckland

Printed and bound in Hong Kong

A CIP catalog record of this book is available from the Library of Congress

ISBN 0-517-15969-4

8 7 6 5 4 3 2 1

http://www.randomhouse.com

Contents

In the Beginning

Steam railway made nations. Countries became more than inaccessible bundles of small locations. Man could see his patriotism expand, experience a broadening of horizons – an extension of his ability to communicate beyond the territorial and language barriers.

Equally, he could more readily fear the advancement of land enemies – enemies who might now come to his neighborhood in days – whereas before the coming of the Ironhorse he might never see a foreigner from birth to death. Some of the first people to expect and fear the coming of steam locomotion were the American Indians. Tales were told of how the Ironhorse would finally wipe out the true inhabitants of America. The land prospectors and the gold-diggers of the "Union" could more readily break through that vast untouched territory, elbowing aside any who tried to stop them.

The insecurity engendered by railway struck not only the American Indian. For more than half a century leading up to World War I the German fatherland suffered national uncertainty as it watched its homeland being hemmed in on all sides by the spreading railway track of France and Austria, like industrious spiders spinning a web that seemed always to converge on Berlin.

This paranoia must have contributed much to the coming "Great War" – Deutschland behaving like a cat in a corner.

The increased speed of travel helped define territories and permitted greater exploration. This linear motivation, given a certain increased rate of speed, makes towns and territories more easily accessible and therefore more heavily populated, more visited, better financed and more efficient. So centers grew and thrived.

I see over my own continent the Pacific railroad surmounting every barrier,
I see continual trains of cars winding along the Platte carrying freight and passengers,
I hear the locomotives rushing and roaring, and the shrill steel whistle,
I hear the echoes, reverberating through the grandest scenery in the world,
Bridging the three or four thousand miles of land travel,
Tying the Eastern to the Western sea...

Walt Whitman - *Passage to India.*

The picture opposite is of a reconstructed 0-6-0 engine built specially for a Yugoslavian movie.

Beyond a given rate of travel and communication the effect disperses and the town is as easily by-passed as it is visited. Whole countries, with the coming of the jet plane and electricity, take on an irrelevance as man spans the globe physically in hours and vocally in seconds. The steam locomotive was the last of the great linear movements, where land was experienced rather than ignored and life could be tracked at a sensual rate.

One man set in motion this world-wide change. A frail twenty-seven-year-old, James Watt altered the face of steam power and its capacity to power man's movement, starting in the academic year of 1763-64 in the Natural Philosophy class of Glasgow University, in Scotland. Watt was a mathematical instrument-maker and was asked to improve the performance of a Newcomen engine which had been developed to demonstrate to students the change of water into steam, half a century before. The boiler of the engine was only large enough to supply steam for a few strokes, and the University required it to function continuously. Watt's task was to find a way of reducing steam consumption and he solved the problem, after one year of work, by adding a separate condenser alongside the boiler. The condenser was exhausted into a vacuum state and the "elastic" steam was drawn in and condensed, thus providing, in one stroke, a system that was able to cut steam consumption by seventy-five percent.

The next step in the evolution of steam locomotion was taken by an Englishman named Richard Trevithick, who in 1804 built the very first steam engine, similar to the old pumping engine with one cylinder, a crank and connecting rod to provide rotary motion, and a large fly-wheel to give continuous motion and avoid stalling. The first journey of this pioneer covered ten miles towing ten tons of iron in five wagons with seventy men aboard! The average speed was two and a half miles per hour!

And after Trevithick came Hedley and "Puffing Billy". This was the very beginning of England's experience of smooth track, steam as train, with the potential to reach the farthest corners of the British Isles.

The year was 1811, the same year that saw the early anti-industrial riots and the machine-breaking Luddites who revolted against losing their jobs to mechanization. It also saw the British banks propping up a dwindling economy and in Europe, Napoleon was crossing the borders into Russia to face the destruction of his "Grande Armeé". In fact, the greater part of the nineteenth century and into the middle of the twentieth saw territorial war on a greater scale than ever before in history, with World War II neatly coinciding with the close of steam locomotion and the opening of the era of the jet plane.

As George Stephenson took on the development of steam locomotion in the early nineteenth century, bullying English railways into life, so also the expansion began in the great lands of America. The white population of this enormous, pioneering country numbered then about five million, all living within an eight-hundred-thousand-square-mile area on one side of the Allegheny Mountains. Beyond this range to the west lay a vast region of unexplored land just waiting to be laid with hard iron track. Towns had already grown up on the wide rivers of the Mississippi, Missouri and Ohio valleys and transport had naturally taken to the water, all running from north to south. But it was soon necessary to establish communications between the lands beyond the Alleghenies and the ports that ranged the Atlantic seaboard.

As early as 1812, a deposition was sent to England to investigate steam potential and it became clear that there was a wide contrast between the potential of the two countries. The English steam barons were cash-rich and their railways needed to cover only relatively small distances with little gradient variation. The Americans had massive land potential as their wealth but with little cash, huge distances to cover and giant leaps through mountainous regions to pioneer. Britain enjoyed a population of some sixteen million people, already quite able to afford railway travel. Public railway was economic and safe whereas by contrast in America it was neither popular nor safe.

The American Central Pacific Railroad, one of the first long-distance lines of steam locomotion, made deals with the Indian tribes of the areas through which the trains would pass, without incident. But the Union Pacific could not hope to do the same as their lines cut across the buffalo trails that were the life-blood of the Cheyennes and Sioux Indians. The Indians would strap large timber logs to the tracks and then kill and scalp those who survived the crash, taking over the contents of the trains. Hundreds of lives were lost before the battle was finally given up.

The French also visited England before setting up their first railway network, starting steam locomotion work mainly to carry coal, passenger railway only beginning in 1844. England continued to be the main pioneering country in steam locomotion and the work of George Stephenson was probably the most significant in making travel cheap, fast and comfortable. His vision extended to cover the whole of Britain with track from city to city and all that remained in the following years was to increase the speed of travel more and more.

On the new American continent the drive for steam improvement took the form of both speed and size. Whereas in Europe, the social development up to the end of the nineteenth century had taken hundreds of years to achieve, in America it all happened much faster, and most of it coincided with the duration of the era of steam locomotion. Between 1790 and 1810 American population figures had increased from four million to just over seven, and doubled thereafter each twenty years until the end of the century. What required two thousand years to develop in Europe occurred rapidly in the emigration of people of all the European races to one vast and extremely rich land.

But not all railway pioneering was so positive and determined. During the early years of German locomotion the people's response was sour and the Bavarian College of Physicians had this to say about the hazards of steam traction:

"The rapid movement (of trains) must inevitably generate in the travelers a brain disease, a special variety of 'delirium furiosum'. *If travelers are nevertheless determined to brave this fearful danger the state must at least protect the onlookers, for otherwise these will be affected with the same brain disease at the sight of the rapidly-running steam wagon. It is therefore necessary to enclose the railway on both sides with a high, tight, broad fence."*

A Professor Kips, also in Bavaria, warned against the steam locomotive, saying that it would affect horse breeding and eventually the great German cavalry would not be strong enough to fight off invaders from other countries. In the event, it wasn't invading cavalry that made Germany paranoid, but invading steam trains.

Between 1836 and 1839 steam railway lines opened in Austria, France, Russia, Belgium, Italy and Holland. However, looked at on a global scale, locomotion track was still heavily concentrated on one small island north of Europe with little or nothing as advanced for many years to come.

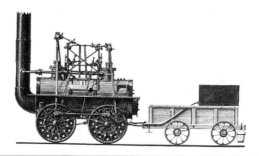

In the early years of European steam, the lines spread across France and Austria, like the web of an industrious spider, seemingly all converging on Berlin, to the chagrin of the new German nation.

The Line Divides

If we view the development of the steam locomotive in the same way as we might look at a natural evolutionary process, it becomes clear that by the middle of the nineteenth century there were two essentially different species which had become established on either side of the Atlantic.

The basic elements of the organism had been established by the 1840s and little change was to occur until the species died out in both countries well over a century later. The creature is, by modern standards, absurdly simple. All it needs is a water boiler, a firebox, cylinders with a drive mechanism to the wheels and track. The food can be anything that will burn and heat the water, be it wood, coal, oil or sugar cane.

This new evolutionary animal first appeared in Britain and it is perhaps no coincidence that it chose this country as its birthplace. For the steam engine England was the Garden of Eden. It was born in its own food trough – the coalmine, and a very high grade coal at that. It was also an environment particularly well suited to its other needs. England was a small country in the first flowering of the Industrial Revolution and there was a desperate need to transport the new commodities.

The growth of the British Empire was at its most vital stage and new markets were bursting to be handled by the ports. The country enjoyed a peak of optimism – the long war with Napoleon had only just ended and the economy was surging upward under Victorian influence. Coal-mines boomed to meet the demands of factories, steel manufacturers, wool and cotton mills and money was readily available for new investment. An experienced work-force already exist-

A typical little British locomotive of the 1860s. By this time both the design parameters and the dimensions of the new invention were pretty much laid down. Essentially, the British made small and very fast locomotives with wheels set within a short and rigid frame. The huge diameter driving wheel was intended for high speeds over excellent tracks. Even in 1860 speeds of over 60 miles an hour became normal. As distances were relatively short only a small tender was needed for water and high grade coal. Yet strangely there was no cab for the notoriously damp and cold English weather.

ed from the construction of the canals to build the railways, the viaducts, the tunnels and the embankments. There was also a new middle-class businessman eager to find new markets at home and abroad in the search for wealth, and to explore the coastal towns and beauty spots of his own country. The resulting spread of track from the 1830s to 1870 created a railway network which remains virtually unchanged today. The engineers and railway companies established, in those early, experimental years, physical parameters which determined both the advantages and disadvantages of British design for the next century and a half.

Tracks were laid smooth, straight and level with as few curves, inclines and irregularities as possible. This allowed small but very fast locomotives, hauling passenger traffic at over sixty miles per hour even in the 1860s. The young British species of that time was distinguished by huge diameter driving wheels, about as out-of-proportion as the old "penny-farthing" bicycle of the same period. The style was intended for speed, with stabilizing wheels within a simple rigid frame. There was no necessity for bogies or swivelling trucks as the curves were gentle

The standard 4-4-0 "American" counterpart was slow, rugged and massive by comparison to the little thoroughbred. Two innovative design features were the coupled driving wheels, giving better traction for steep gradients and the forward swivel "truck" or four-wheel "bogie" which could adapt to the regular pioneer track with its tight curves. Everything was big: the boiler, the firebox, the tender and the massive smoke stack for repressing sparks as the early models were all wood burners. A closed and often ornate cab completed the North American breed.

and could accommodate the short engine frames. As few inclines were encountered, the traction disadvantages of the huge diameter wheels were not considered a problem.

Yet these early physical limitations of height, rail-gauge and width of rolling stock, firmly established by 1860, also meant that tunnels, cuttings and the width beside the track severely limited the growth potential of any future organism. By comparison, the later examples of locomotives in America or the giants in France and Germany had much greater room for growth even though easy access to high grade coal and level tracks put Britain ahead in the initial years.

On the other side of the Atlantic there were no such space restrictions. In fact, there was too much space. Locomotives and carriages were much taller and wider as there were no tunnels, cuttings or overhead lines. Tracks tended to go around obstacles rather than blasting through them. Gradients were often gruelling and curves far beyond the wildest imagination of British engineers. In fact, the early imports from England often found themselves coming off the irregular tracks. This failure of the little British thoroughbred to adapt to the rough conditions of the new world led American engineers to create a rugged species better suited to the pioneer conditions of their own lands. Robert Stephenson had suggested an engine with a single pair of drive wheels and a forward swivel truck which could better adapt to the rough and curvy track. Within less than a decade a new wheel arrangement made its debut. The driving wheels were coupled with a second pair insuring far better traction – the 4-4-0 was born. "The American" was the most successful of all steam locomotives with over twenty-five thousand engines built before the end of the century.

Models could be bought over the counter like Ford cars today with the later examples built in a simple and rugged way, boasting average speeds of twenty-five miles per hour on light irregular track. The railroad companies had neither the cash nor the manpower to build the massive foundations which England boasted. The American Civil War had shown the importance of railroads but it had unhappily swallowed up the young, able-bodied men who could have laid the tracks.

One fascinating divergence that differentiated the British from the American species was in the construction of the closed and often ornate cab occupied by the driver. Perhaps it was as much for protection against the warring Indians as against the weather but an English counterpart did not appear until the 1870s. It might be an indication of how railway companies viewed their staff. To drive a locomotive in the cold sleet of an English winter at over sixty miles per hour with no overhead protection does somewhat belie the otherwise elegant design of what was then the fastest steam engine in the world.

The construction and foundations of the railway track itself had a very particular effect both on the British and North American innovators of steam locomotion. In Britain the powerful influence of early locomotive engineers was to be felt in the building of under-track structures. Engineers insisted on straight and level tracks with few curves and gradients, built on beds of compacted gravel or even constructed with brick and stone. A great deal of attention was given to high quality surveying and good drainage. The purpose of this painstaking effort was to ensure smooth running, as much for the benefit of the precious engines as for the passengers. Good foundations minimized wear and tear on the rolling stock and subsequent maintenance costs, and had a profound effect on the whole design of British steam locomotion. Engines were built as rigidly as the foundations on which they ran, with compact, short wheelbases carried within small frames with springing on each pair of wheels.

British contractors, unlike their American counterparts, were fortunate to have first-class labor forces readily available. These skilled men had had long experience with the building of embankments and cuttings. It seems fitting that such a workforce should come from the earlier main transport system in England – the canal. Canals had long carried the major heavy traffic throughout the British Isles and the advent of the new steam locomotive spelled their demise. The "navigators" of the canals became the "navvies" of the railways, commanding high incomes for their work. Operating in huge "elite" teams they completed projects at an incredible speed

Top left are two pioneer railway workers in the new lands of America.

Below – a scene that would wet the eyes of any Camden Town, London dweller – the original cutting made in 1840 using the high-class labor of the time, men who had built the old canals.

and it is testimony to such workers that the British Rail network as it is still today, spread across the whole nation in just thirty years.

Economically, at that time, Britain had moved into an era of intense speculation. The newly founded prosperous class of businessman was looking for a long-term investment and many competing railway companies were founded on this need. The expanding railway network connected local interests with the main centers of industry and commerce: the coalmines, steel companies, the wool and cotton mills, the ports and the new markets of the colonies and protectorates.

The tiny compact center of a British Empire at its peak was the perfect environment for the evolution of such a revolutionary machine. Yet in America the situation was completely different. The emerging railroad companies were quite simply short of cash. Few people were prepared to invest in the unproven new machine although many could see the possibilities once the huge continent was opened up. The territory, though, was so vast and the cost of laying track in the same way as the British had done, was out of the question. Railway lines had to be simple and cheap and one of the biggest drawbacks was a lack of man-power. No money and no men! It has to be remembered that the greater part of America's advance into locomotion happened in the 1870s – after the American Civil War. By this time the British railway network was virtually complete and England had suffered none of the disadvantages of a slaughtered youth.

These problems were made considerably worse by the advent of the gold-rush – all the able-bodied men left were panning for gold. The labor available for the railway companies were, to put it mildly, a wild bunch. Ex-Civil War veterans from both the Union and Confederate camps, Irish immigrants who had just arrived in search of fortune, ex-

Below – dormitory cars for the construction workers in America on the St Pauls Michigan and Milwaukee Railway in the 1880s.

On the right – an engine plate from the Schenectady Works of the American Locomotive Company, on an engine in Ghana.

convicts, gamblers, farmers, drifters, ex-canalmen and later even immigrant Chinese were all conscripted into the work-gangs. It was this rugged "army" which managed to lay the largest railroad complex on this planet. Not only did they have to lay at least a mile of track a day but they were often required to defend themselves against hostile Indians who saw the Ironhorse as a symbol of the fall of their great tribes. The track was as rough as the "Iron men" who laid it. And it was this light, irregular track which determined the design of the "American Standard" 4-4-0 and the subsequent, simple and sturdy breeds which followed.

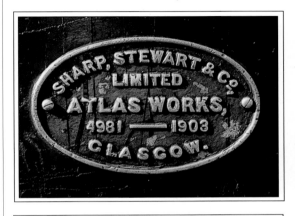

Manufacturers' engine plates have a poetry uniquely their own. They seem to express the poignancy of head stones in windswept graveyards. Yet these are in fact the birth plates, and their interest includes their final destination. To find an "Atlas Works" name-plate from Glasgow in Glasgow is one thing, but the same plate found in the Amazon jungle is altogether another. Finding, unexpectedly, an engine plate from say the legendary Schenectady workshops of the USA, in the North African desert is a reminder of just how much the steam engine has altered the face of the world.

It is easy to forget in this casual age of communications and information that only one hundred and fifty years ago the steam engine was looked upon with as much excitement and opportunity as the space shuttle is today. It has earned its place as the first leap in the communication efforts of modern man.

It shares that place with the telegraph which appeared only five years later, and these two innovations exploded man's awareness of both space and time. If there was a point at which the world began to change into a global village it had to be one hundred and fifty years ago when the first locomotives trundled down a north-of-England track into the beginning of the golden age of travel.

Top left – the work-plate of Sharp, Stewart & Co. All these plates were evidence of the way railway spread across the world – many of them where found in the most remote areas.

Bottom left – an engine plate from one of the greatest engineering companies – Greenwood & Batley of Leeds in the north of England – ever occupied in machine tool making.

The top right plate is from the Kitson Company of Leeds, one of the most celebrated British engine manufacturers.

The bottom right picture of this foursome is an engine plate from the famous Beyer Peacock Company of Manchester, England.

The Inheritors

Perhaps one of the greatest contributions that the British Empire conferred upon its unsuspecting colonies and protectorates was the railway and its handmaiden, the timetable. In the pre-war maps of the world, the amount of pink-colored land of the then vast British Empire encompassed a very sizeable chunk of the atlas. Almost half of the world's population had been touched by the lines that are colored pink on the maps, each long tendril designating iron track on which the ubiquitous British steam locomotive ran. Yet so many of the lands were really unsuited to the little thoroughbred engines of tiny island origin. As the colonies began to take over the reigns of their own government many of the larger territories looked to the big, tough and simple designs of America for their long-distance passenger and main line freight traffic.

Yet to see the little British Bulldog 0-6-0 side-tankers working alongside huge American or German-giant mainliners somewhere in the plains of India or the lowlands of Turkey, indicates how the evolution of steam locomotion divided so clearly into two parts. Like the two ends of a magical, colored spectrum, the railroad down which the two countries traveled had very different requirements and their varied influences on the other developing nations enriched the whole era of steam.

In India, during the Raj, the first locomotives were, of course, British. During the 1920s and 30s, the standard Indian designs were found to be totally unsatisfactory for the gruelling long-distance hauls. During the Second World War the tough US Army Transport Corps engines found their way to India to help supplies for the Burma campaign. These simple

and highly adaptable machines perfectly suited Indian requirements and when the war was ended, even before independence, orders were given to American engineers to update the main line services in both wide and meter gauge lines.

An example of the American style seen in India was the 755WP class 4-6-2, run on the standard express passenger lines of the wide gauge. The essential beauty of this American machine was its rugged simplicity — its ability to haul enormous train loads packed with humanity across the vast plains of India.

In fact the 4-6-2 was the last of the express engines to be built in the USA, yet they gave way to an incredible heritage. Both the Russians and the Chinese railway builders modelled much of their massive rolling stock on the American designs.

Perhaps, technically, the ultimate expression of North American steam locomotion was the "Niagara." Few engines in the world could be said to be perfect, but the Niagara – a huge 4-8-4 – was about as close to the perfection of steam as it is possible to get. It was certainly the last really new passenger engine, capable of running the distance between New York and Chicago day after day without stop.

Opposite page – on the Black Sea coast of Turkey, molten waste is picked up from the factories and tipped down the slag banks by trucks hauled with a Newcastle built 0-6-0 saddle tank of classic design from the British builders, Robert Stephenson and Hawthorn. The steel works from which this waste was brought was Turkey's first on the line from Irmak to Zonguldak, originally opened by Ataturk himself in the 1930s.

Above – three of the American war machines, hardy, powerful and long-lasting engines built for the US Army Transportation Corps during World War II. These engines formed almost their own design genre and can be identified by their capacity to survive in arduous conditions. They ended their days as industrial pilots around Calcutta.

Over on the following two pages is a wonderful picture depicting reconstructed 4-4-0s as they would have been on the ceremony of the "Golden Spike" where Union Pacific met Central Pacific on the great drive across America.

The

What was it the Engines said,
Pilots touching – head to head
Facing on the single track,
Half a world behind each back?

Once upon a time in America three devices were created that would alter the entire face of the land and enable one nation to overthrow another.

In 1835 the revolver was invented, in 1837 the telegraph began operating, and in that same decade, the steam locomotive set forth on its track to provide the new people of America with fast transport. These three mechanical devices, combined, created such a force for change that the American Indian inevitably had to give way to the pioneers.

Of these three steps made by mankind in his conquest of the West, the steam locomotive was by far the greatest. Not only the American Indians feared the coming of the Ironhorse but also those who had made a little progress into this vast untouched land of unequalled riches.

The riverboatmen with their trade along the wide rivers, the canalmen and wagoners who had struggled to make an impact on the discovery of gold and silver and other precious metals from the ground – all feared the coming

States

Said the Union: "Don't reflect, or
I'll run over some Director."
Said the Central: "I'm Pacific;
But, when riled, I'm quite terrific.
Yet today we shall not quarrel,
Just to show these folks this moral,
How two Engines -- in their vision --
Once have met without collision."
Breat Harte

of the great steam railway, for its power to command was to be responsible almost totally for the way the developing States would grow.

Right up to the 1850s the few white settlers had made very little impact on the vast country of America. Their small, slow wagons and their inefficient steam boats fought an unequal battle against land and river, and left little evidence of their presence.

"We do not ride on the railroad; it rides upon us. Did you ever think what those sleepers are that underlie the railroad? Each one is a man, an Irishman, or a Yankee man."
Henry David Thoreau

The Ironhorse was certainly not responsible for as many deaths as the revolver, but those who traveled through the rough country aboard the locomotives of the 1850s and later, used the revolver and the telegraph to great effect in changing the country.

Builder of Nations

Everything involved in locomotion had its impact. Even the simple fact of the different gauges, while they remained different, contributed to the growth of towns. Each time a rail gauge changed, it was necessary for the train-load of passengers to off-load in order to board another gauge train. In this way passengers became settlers as they dallied in one place or another, or brought trade with them that would otherwise have remained aboard the train.

As in Britain before the advent of the steam locomotive, there was no standard time in America. Right up to 1883 a clock on Long Island would show correctly the "mean solar" time for its location but would be ahead of a clock in Newark, New Jersey. The Newark clock would be ahead of a clock in Trenton, N.J. which in turn would also be ahead of a clock in Philadelphia. And so on across the country.

By the time steam locomotion was a regular feature of American life "mean solar" or "local civil" time was not sufficient. Standard time was created, as it operates today, dividing the country up into the four meridians: Eastern Standard, Central Standard, Mountain Standard and Pacific Standard times. As Canada developed, with its wider span from east to west, two further meridians were established: Atlantic Standard on one end and Yukon Standard on the other. Alaska added Alaska Standard and Nome Standard times.

We now take for granted a planet divided into twenty-four time zones, one hour each, and automatically consider in our minds that from Europe to the west coast of America, one sleeps while the other has tea! All this fantasy began with a puff of smoke.

America tested the locomotive still further with the Civil War which, so soon after Independence, the country was already fighting. For supplies and men a steam train was hard to beat, and the Standard American 4-4-0 at the beginning of the 1860s rose in price from around five thousand dollars to around fourteen thousand in four years.

On the positive side, the war standardized the gauges and through the nervousness of President Lincoln, who feared reprisals from the friends of the defeated Confederates in Europe who might enter America from the west coast, the Union Pacific Railroad was built.

With the problem of the Civil War still evident, marauding Indians and the government's financial difficulties, the track across the state of Nebraska was hugely handicapped. In addition, materials for the construction had to be shipped by sea, and there was no Panama Canal in the 1860s so that the trip around the tip of Cape Horn was fifteen thousand miles long. But once underway the track was laid at the rate of some thousand miles in the first three years, and it was in this era that Chinese laborers replaced immigrant Irish labor and became the first Chinese to set up home in the States.

The methods employed by the railroad companies to attract immigrant workers into the hazardous track-laying work may be seen from advertisements of the time, which hardly reflected the facts of a life which was extremely tough, and might result in a scalping. Meanwhile the railway moguls such as Vanderbilt and Crocker made vast fortunes in this early time of growth.

Left – a true, living "Iron Horse" of the year 1883 – the faithful animal that helped construct the railways with the gangs laying track on the first American transcontinental railway.

Opposite page – blazing new trails in the "Old West" and the south, a construction scene during the early years of railroads.

Opening up a Continent

O'Hare Airport in the city of Chicago is today the busiest airport in the American continent, perhaps in the world, and since transport became an important aspect of human activity, Chicago has always been a place where travel converged. Aircraft leave O'Hare once every three seconds, and in the middle years of American steam-locomotion growth the center to quickly become the most busy was Chicago. As this development rose to a peak there were no fewer than twenty-two different main line railways that served the city, with through trains to every part of the United States. The lines converge on Chicago like the spokes of a wheel – to the south come the Chicago and Eastern Illinois lines, the Illinois Central, the Wabash, the Gulf, Mobile and Ohio lines. From the east are the Baltimore and Ohio, and the Chesapeake and Ohio, formed from the Michigan Central, and the "Big Four." Going to the west of south we find the services to and from the west coast – the Atchison, Topeka and Santa Fe, and the Chicago, Rock Island and Pacific, then the Chicago, Burlington and Quincy. Due west come the Chicago and North Western, the Chicago Great Western, the Chicago Milwaukee, St Paul and Pacific, and the Illinois Central. Traveling north there are tight groups of lines, most of which head for Milwaukee before they spread across the north. Here are the Chicago and North Western, the Milwaukee, and the Minneapolis, St Paul and Sault Ste Marie.

This whole wheel around Chicago had to be connected and the whole development of railway in America had to take into account a great many requirements which would eventually result in what we see today. Freight transfer railways that extended in arcs connecting all the various spokes of this wheel, provided the interchanges needed between the converging lines.

Each of these "interlopers" was set up by individual companies like the "Indiana Harbor Belt" and the "Chicago Union Transfer", also operating in some cases suburban passenger railways. There was also the Chicago "Loop" or "Elevated" the remains of which still existed until fairly recently. In those days there were six railway stations in Chicago with the extreme inconvenience of no connecting railway between them, so that passengers had to get off the train at one station and travel to another before being able to catch the next train. This was also so with the freight which must have discouraged many from using the railway at all, until the "Belt Railway Company" was founded in the early 1900s. By the 1920s the company was handling no less than six thousand wagons a day!

Left – a typical Union Pacific poster that could be found all over the world to attract labor to America for the railroad drive. Conditions were never as they were made out to be.

Opposite page – one of the most dramatic pictures – the legendary "American" – an engine that could almost be bought over the counter like a Ford car today.

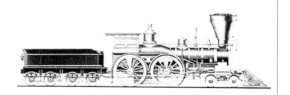

The American Pioneer

— First Fruit Train to Leave California —

The Promised Land

Opposite page:
Top left – a scene at Wyoming Station, engine 23 on Main Track. With antlers on the headlight and diamond stack, the engine has been shined bright.
Top right – a typical "American" 4-4-0 of the late 19th century. Bottom left – the first solid train to leave California, in 1884, the trucks laden with fruit. And (bottom right) the first train to operate between Stockton and Fresno – a 55 ton Baldwin – October 5th 1896.

Above – a typical kettle used in the early days of railroading to supply drinking water to passengers. Below are the vast crowds of immigrant workers boarding a new train bound along the newest of lines.

Meet Ya in Chicago

The famous Chicago "Union Stock Yards", during the late 1880s, were estimated to have handled three million head of cattle, three million sheep and six million pigs – telling us a lot about the meat consumption of the United States at that time.

Competition continued to be a major feature of steam railway into the twentieth century. As a natural consequence of development, when man finds a way to travel faster then the next step is a desire to travel faster still. This tendency created the success of steam locomotion but also ended it as other forms of transport became increasingly fast and efficient. The beginning of the speed growth was in the 1890s. In the USA on the competitive routes between New York and Philadelphia the fifty-five-point-seven-mile trip from New York to Trenton could be covered already in just over one hour including stops. By the end of the 1890s, when in Britain the legendary "race to the north" on lines between London and Edinburgh had proved the capability of steam locomotion as a fast business-maker, speeds of seventy miles per hour were common. Higher speeds, greater comfort and lower fares made the railway an establishment, particularly the United Kingdom which was still somewhat ahead of the rest of the world.

But in 1893 and through the turn of the centu-

ry, speed-fever became the vogue, especially in America. It was in this era of locomotion that the one-hundred-mile-per-hour peak was claimed for the first time. The "Empire State Express", first on track in 1891, reached a claimed speed of one hundred and two point eight miles per hour on May 9th 1893, between Syracuse and Buffalo. Only two days later the same engine claimed one hundred and twelve and a half miles per hour.

Some years later, when speed checks had become more precise, it was made clear that these claimed speeds were probably about twenty miles per hour short, but nevertheless the trend towards speed was very much a central issue. All that remained now, before the decline of steam locomotion, was the great increase in size.

Before the close of the nineteenth century, it was theoretically possible to travel around the world by steam. Today, package tours might call such a trip – "Stoke-up and See the World!" From San Francisco to China and Suez by steam-powered boat, from Suez to Alexandria by rail, from Alexandria to France by water, from France to Liverpool by locomotive and steam boat, and from Liverpool to New York by water, then by rail across the continent to San Francisco by steam locomotive. Steam all the way.

"Man's genius seems materialized in the Iron Horse, and no one can look upon a locomotive of today without having a feeling come over him that is akin to awe."

Golden Age of Speed

Thus, steam had effected its task — it had defined national boundaries and it had shrunk the world. Coincidentally it was also at the end of the nineteenth century that steam began its decline, soon to be replaced by diesel, the motor vehicle and the airplane. But before it was finally over, the proud American people who had bound the world with "links of iron" would continue to build some of the largest land-based vehicles in the history of the planet.

In 1904 the Union Pacific Railroad was running the "Pacific" 4-6-2 at a weight of almost one hundred tons without tender, and in the same period the Baldwin Locomotive Company of Philadelphia built seventy 2-10-2 type locomotives known as the "Santa Fe" locomotives for the Atchison, Topeka and Santa Fe Railroad — each engine alone weighing in at one hundred and twenty tons, and with a full load of coal and water in a tender, over two hundred tons.

The Pacific 4-6-2 continued to be one of the world's finest passenger-hauling engines right through into the 1940s, by which time locomotives such as the "Hudson" type 4-6-4 could track over nine hundred miles from Chicago to Colorado at average speeds of eighty miles per hour with altitudes of seven thousand feet above sea level and pulling train weights over one thousand tons.

Finally, among the Union Pacific's "Big Boys" the largest locomotives of all time were reached, with engine and tender measuring one hundred and twenty feet and a total weight of five hundred and twenty tons.

By then diesel was already a viable form of railway transport and the engine that had straddled the world was close to its last service.

Above — a classic pair of engines — the right hand being the famous 999 which made, the recorded fastest run of 112.5 MPH, lying alongside the streamlined version of the New York Central's famous J3 "Hudson." The casing of this latter engine was designed by Henry Dreyfus.

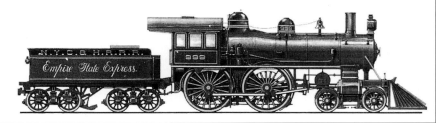

The Giants

Top left – the Challenger
4-6-6-4 – the largest, strongest,
heaviest and most powerful
locomotive which ever handled
express passenger trains.

Opposite – an example of the
beautifully streamlined Norfolk
and Western 4-8-4 express
coaling up.

Local Heroes

Opposite and this page – the K-36 2-8-2 Denver & Rio Grande Western Railroad engines – locomotives that ran the "last proper steam railroad in the USA."

These beautifully preserved locomotives are typical of the local trains which had long and faithful service in isolated areas in the USA. Often they were engines which had been retired from the big main line services to find a new life on smaller company lines.

Penultimate Express-ion

Two engines worthy of special mention in the American development of steam – trains that formed the penultimate force – were the "Hiawatha" and the Class GS-4 4-8-4.

Fleet of foot was Hiawatha" – wrote Longfellow and he might easily have written it of this incredible steam express, inspired by the traffic between Chicago and the twin cities of St Paul and Minneapolis. The railway company actually ordered this engine for travel at one hundred miles per hour and more to cover a distance of four hundred and twelve miles in six and a half hours. The Hiawatha developed three thousand horsepower and hauled nine coaches to travel the distance with five intermediate stops and fifteen speed restrictions of less than fifty miles per hour – still managing to reduce the intended six and a half hours by a further fifteen minutes.

The GS-4 type 4-8-4 worked the very long passenger route between Los Angeles and San Francisco – four hundred and seventy miles with one in forty-five gradients and the trains hauled weighed in at five hundred and sixty-eight tons – twelve carriages! The train was known as the "Daylight" express and over the runs it averaged forty-eight and a half miles per hour which, considering the difficult gradients and tight curvatures, was fast. Unique amongst express trains of the time the Daylight express also operated with electro-pneumatic brake systems – common today, but not in the 1930s.

These two trains were the fastest North American steam express trains of all times.

The Late Great Expresses

A S-3 class 2-8-4 engine of the
"Nickel Plate Road" or the New
York, Chicago & St Louis which
never went to New York – 367 tons.

Streamlined elegance and
speed, the Norfolk and Western
4-8-4.

The biggest of the giants – the
A5 class 4-8-4 that hauled the
"Alaskan" out of Minneapolis
in the 1950s.

The ultimate steam locomotive,
as some would call it, the
"Niagara" 4-8-4 of the New
York Central Railroad.

The Last of the Giants

The M3 "Yellowstone" 2-8-8-4, engines that pulled the heaviest steam-hauled trains anywhere in the world on regular operation – on the Duluth, Missabe & Iron Range Railroad.

The "Allegheny" 2-6-6-6 ran the Chesapeake & Ohio line – again, one of the most powerful ever built.

The Union Pacific 4-6-6-4 "Challenger" – the largest, strongest, heaviest and most powerful of all the express-hauling engines.

Union Pacific's "Big Boy", the most evocative of names – with a total weight of 539 tons.

Canada

Top left and left – the 4-6-4 No. 2860, now preserved and running on the British Columbia Railway in Canada.

Opposite page – Canadian Pacific's 1246, passenger express engine.

As a typical example of how steam railway forced the definitions of national territories, the first proposals for a railway in Canada immediately brought forward the question of where the new American lands would end and the existing British Empire territories of Canada would begin. The lands of Canada, in the 1830s, consisting only of a few settlements along the St Lawrence river, needed some efficient means of transport between Quebec and the ports of the Atlantic seaboard in the British Colonies. The first plans foundered pretty quickly because the Americans objected to the line, fearing it might pass through US territory. The intended line was to have been a five hundred mile long track supported by the British government – first with a survey supplement of ten thousand pounds and then later with funding of the track-laying itself.

This was no small project for the start of a Canadian railway system but the territorial problems delayed it for a further twenty years. Lesser railway developments to and from Montreal did go ahead however, supported and entrained by Stephenson engines.

The greatest railway in the world was eventually set in motion within the territories of Canada – the Canadian Pacific. Political considerations once again took a hand in the development of this railway, but in this case with a positive result. The American, John Macdonald, first premier to the Dominion of Canada was very eager for the two colonies of British Columbia and Vancouver Island to join the confederation of the eastern provinces that had formed under the British North American Act of 1867, and under this act an agreement was made between the two provinces to built a railway within ten years of the date of their union.

In fact it was not until nearly fourteen years later that the Canadian Pacific Railroad actually got under way. Political problems in Canada continued and Macdonald went out of office until 1881 when he finally managed to start the

National and Pacific

Left – the "Selkirk" class
2-10-4, a ten-coupled
locomotive used in most parts
of the world for freight
movement.
Below – the luxurious
"Trans-Canada" leaves Windsor
Station, Montreal for
Vancouver, 1929.

project by financing the operation through private enterprise rather than continuing with government backing. Securing the President of the Bank of Montreal as the head of a group of businessmen, he undertook the formation of the company that was to build the railroad and then run it.

The route of this first major, trans-continental railroad in Canada had by necessity to get across the great Rocky Mountains, and the surveyor who had been given the task of finding the most practical way through this part of the journey suggested the Yellowhead Pass, which to the delight of Macdonald, did not need any exceptional gradients. But here again political considerations caused problems. Although the Yellowhead Pass might have been the simplest route it was not territorially the most convenient: it left too broad a strip of land between the proposed railway and the borders of the United States. American settlers could theoretically plant themselves there, where they were not wanted, between Winnipeg and the west. The one alternative, the Crows Nest Pass, was at the other end of the scale – too close to the US borders for comfort.

The "Royal Hudson" class 4-6-4
of the Canadian Pacific
Railroad, now in preserved
running order – an 88 ton
weight, hauls passenger trains
in British Columbia.

The 4-8-4 of the Canadian
National Railway – one engine,
already withdrawn, was chalked
with the following verse: *"In
days gone by this junk pile now,
Was a grand sight to behold, On
threads of steel it dashed along,
Like a Knight in armor bold..."*

As often in railway development, the plans only got underway because of one big personality – in this case an American named J.J. Hill. Hill simply pushed the situation into action by hiring a surveyor and engineers to get on with the job, surveying a new route through the Rockies and making plans for an entire two thousand mile route of the Canadian Pacific Railway – all to be completed in three years.

Once Macdonald had formed the syndicate and Hill had set the ball in motion, then there came a man whose name would reverberate down through railway history as one of the great names of the genre – in many ways even as great as Brunel himself. This man was Sir William Van Horne and he became the general manager of the Canadian Pacific Railway in 1881 at the age of thirty-nine, with the task of completing that which his promoters had proposed.

The route was finally settled to take the course along the lakeside north of Lake Superior, all Canadian and away from any American territorial influence. Thus began Van Horne's extraordinary task – blasting through solid rock with non-existent communications and labor provided mostly by boat and spread out over six hundred miles of work line. Special boats were built for Van

Horne in Glasgow and gunpowder factories established along the shore line. Van Horne, in his directorship even had to deal with the sort of problems that might still be associated with small businesses when they are struggling to get on their feet – cash ran out and of course the work crews needed paying. Van Horne used a device to solve this one that small businesses might know well – he issued the workers with checks knowing they would not reach a bank to cash them for several months!

This financial deprivation along with the incredible geographical problems continued to dog the work of Van Horne right up to the time in 1885 when the Royal Assent in England was given to a government funding for the remains of the great Canadian Pacific Railroad.

Van Horne left nothing of his work without personal care and attention, very often walking through the most rugged forest and mountain routes on foot, through rain and snow and the worst conditions to make sure that all went the way he planned. The result was yet another example of the determination of one single man to get the job done, regardless of the difficulties.

British Isles

The British Isles have to be congratulated as the very first to see and take advantage of the potential of steam locomotion. Before the coming of railway, Britain was made up of small, sleepy, farming communities with no standardized time, no national travel or communication network, and no facility for expanding its industrial or business potential even across such a small area. Stage-coach travel was expensive – out of the range of the pocket of ordinary people. In any event the roads were difficult, and travel by horse slow and laborious, so that the ordinary citizen rarely, if ever, moved more than a few miles from his home. It sometimes seems odd that prior to the beginning of the nineteenth century Britain was simply a series of small communities, often ruled by local barons or squires and with no contact with Parliament or the King. Railways brought a sudden awareness of wider boundaries and also brought huge changes in the form of industry, factories, trade, fast-growing cities and wealth, and – perhaps more important than all this – the opportunity for individuals to travel. The Liverpool and Manchester Railway, initially conceived for the transport of goods, was overwhelmed with passenger interest, and new coaches had to be ordered quickly and in large numbers to accommodate the demand. The services offered in Britain were at first very varied, and one of the biggest reasons for this was the Victorian class structure. It is fine to propose that everyone brings upon himself the fate that he deserves but the Victorian English took

this philosophy to extremes, running their entire lives on the basis that the rich deserved the services of the rich and the poor deserved the rubbish left over. The railways upheld this in their traveling arrangements, with superior first-class travel at one end of the scale and appalling conditions for the engine driver at the other. Improvements happened slowly and some railway companies were better than others, passengers developing loyalty to their own railway lines which, in some cases, has lasted even until today. One of the other major factors which affected this growth of the railway was time-keeping. Part of any railway service today is the way it arranges its timetables and you will always find someone who enjoys complaining about how the train is never on time, either leaving or arriving. In the early to mid-nineteenth century time became the distance between two railway stations. Before the tracks were laid there were hundreds of different times in Britain because nobody needed to know what time it was anywhere except in their own locality. However, once it became possible to make an appointment with a business associate one hundred miles away there suddenly emerged the necessity for it to be the same there as here, and so the train timetable established standardized time-keeping. Station clocks were set each morning by telegraphic communication of "Railway time" – clocks needed to work and passengers stood on platforms staring continuously at their pocket watches. The new linear society had begun.

1830   1840   1850   1860

Opposite page – a 4-6-0 No. 75078 in Mytholmes Cutting in England.

Above – a typical Devon, England scene before the removal of everything steam-powered – the cross-barred gate would forever be leaned on to watch the "puffer" go by.

Left – these maps indicate the way the British Isles developed its railway system between 1830 and 1860 – even today, a network of this size and capacity could not be built faster.

It all began with Black Gold

Without coal it is entirely possible that steam locomotion might never have emerged as the most viable form of transport. Coal is, and was, simple to transport, easy to burn and long lasting enough to provide the power for a compact machine in transit. Britain was very rich in coal and this may have triggered the early development of steam. Prior to steam, coal had often been transported by horse and cart and this, even from the very earliest days, determined the width of rail track. Steam railway therefore not only used coal for fuel but permitted the rapid transport of coal to all other industries that needed it.

Cities grew around their railway stations and the entire belief in "progress" was tied into the natural sciences which almost replaced the Church in its power over mankind. All phenomena was seen as derived from energy and matter and even Darwin's theory of evolution was linked to progress. The steam locomotive was the perfect child of this overall industrial philosophy – after all you could not only believe in what you were doing, in the effect you were having on the world as an industrious businessman, but you could make a fortune at it too.

The steam engine, as it derived its birth from the fuel in the earth, also took its place in a heritage which dated back thousands of years – railway track. In Babylon, around 3000 BC, grooves were cut in the ground, in parallel lines of stone blocks, forming the very first known railway tracks. The inside edges of the "rail" lines was a measurement of four feet and eight inches – the average width of a cart-horse. The cart-horse therefore determined the width of the "rails" between which it would travel and then, of course, the width of the cart it would pull.

Railway lines had also existed in the German states during the Middle Ages and made their first appearance in England during the sixteenth century, slowly growing in the mining areas, ironworks and later as feeders to canals over the next two centuries. During the latter part of the eighteenth century there were also tramlines with flanged plate rails which facilitated smooth-wheeled wagons that could also travel along the public road. All these railways were laid to a variety of gauges but generally between four feet and five feet in width – still the width of a horse and cart.

Above – a typical colliery scene in England during the early 19th century where small steam engines hauled the coal.

Right – a photograph taken in 1900 of a surviving horse-drawn carriage on rails. It was these horse-widths that defined the first regular rail gauges – 4ft 8in.

Opposite page – a double-header hauls a huge load of coal in the north of England at a time when steam was still functioning in the colliery networks.

Century of Progress

Railway gauges were virtually standardized by Parliament after the first major lines of the Liverpool and Manchester Railway in September 1830 – at four feet, eight and a half inches.

Most railway work in the early nineteenth century was still done by horses, of course, partly because of the economics of building huge mechanical monsters but also because of human resistance. Imagine living in a time when a friendly horse would snuffle at the front of a railway cart or carriage, chewing lazily on a bag of grits – there was pleasure and no danger in gently stroking the muzzle of this driving machine. The contrast between this familiar sight and some large metal animal that puffed huge billows of black smoke, making a terrible explosive sound as it boiled up, must have been dramatic enough to put the average man of the early 1800s right off travel.

The very earliest steam locomotives were seen around 1812 and were produced for the colliery lines. The "Blucher", built by George Stephenson in 1814, was constructed to fit the four-foot-eight-inch gauge of the Killingworth Colliery line and those lines connected with it, and when the Stockton and Darlington line was planned in 1821 Stephenson was again the engineer who persuaded the planners to use the same gauge.

Passenger railways at this time were still horse-drawn with the same gauge widths designed for the average horse. The rails themselves were in these cases supported by stone blocks rather than cross sleepers so that the hard-working animals didn't continuously trip over the struts.

Stephenson figured as one of the most significant pioneers throughout all railway development in Britain and when Parliament chose him to regulate and engineer the new railway link of thirty miles between Liverpool and Manchester, he established the four-foot-eight-and-a-half-inch gauge there too.

The above scene was taken in the British Preston Docks in Lancashire where a stud of saddle tanks remained until the end of British industrial steam. The same engine type can be seen (opposite page) – a sixteen-inch cylinder engine, class 18. The engine pictured above was built in 1934 and the engine opposite in 1955, both by Bagnalls of Stafford, neither of which survived long after the pictures were taken.
The church spire seen across the slag dump evokes the clash which came when the scientific epoch was challenged by religious leaders 150 years ago.

The Black Country

Steam railways, though excellent for travel and transporting goods, had an adverse effect on the countryside, on people and on air itself.

Anyone who has traveled across the Ghats which divide Bombay from the southern roads or rails of India in the past few years, will have undoubtedly noticed that it is necessary to protect the eyes and mouth against the fumes and smoke, for fear of asphyxiation. A large black and threatening cloud hangs over the outskirts of this area and just recently dominates the skyline to a distance of about ten miles around the city. In London during the early fifties the fog or smog which fell over the entire city actually killed hundreds of people and eventually initiated the laws against burning coal in fireplaces and industrial sites. The exhaust fumes from cars and trucks in Bombay and the surrounding regions are largely responsible for the intense pollution, and the smog in London was caused by both car fumes, industrial waste and the black smoke that poured out of steam locomotives. A world totally dominated by steam trains during the late eighteenth and early nineteenth centuries meant blackened gardens, vegetables and flowers for anyone unfortunate enough to live near a railway line.

It is usual to look back with sentimentality on those days of the magnificent steam locomotive and easy to forget the pollution it caused.

The three pictures on this spread were all taken at the same colliery network in Ayrshire, Scotland at the Pennyvenie mine, one of the last strongholds of British Industrial steam. The engines were Andrew Barclay tank engines – standard 16in cylinder saddle tanks. The top picture on this page illustrates a tank at rest between duties during shunting operations while the shot below was taken directly after the engine had left the Pennyvenie mine. On the opposite page is a saddle tank in the colliery yard – with the winding gear of the colliery in the background – while the engine waits for coal to pass from the washery into the wagons.

First and Last

Below – an industrial 0-4-0 saddle tank at a power station in the English Midlands struggling to reverse a line of heavy wagons.

Below are two industrial tank locomotives working in the eastern valley of South Wales in the historic iron town of Blaenavon. The left engine is "Toto" and on the right "Nora."

Opposite page – the industrial age blackened the landscape for over a century and a half. Now many of the iron and coal works are abandoned and the landscape has gently renewed itself, as can be seen as this last 0-6-0 saddle tanker passes on.

War of the Gauges

Although the standard track gauge of four feet and eight and a half inches became established in Britain fairly early, there was one, very major divergence from this. This was the broad gauge track of the Great Western Railway which had been designed by the brilliant engineer, Isambard Kingdom Brunel. At five o'clock on Friday 20th May, 1892 the very last broad gauge train – seven foot-and-one-quarter-inch track – left Paddington Station. The train was hauled by the legendary "Iron Duke" class locomotive and after its last journey from London the tracks on which it moved were narrowed to the standard gauges. The great broad gauge railway experiment was at an end.

There had been a continuous debate concerning the advantages and disadvantages of broad or narrow gauge railway and Brunel was at the end of the controversy, always supporting the wide gauge for trunk lines. Broad gauge was held to have great advantages for speed, safety and comfort whereas on the other hand it was expensive to lay and maintain and thought to be ridiculous in a country, intensively industrialized, where through-traffic needed to be compact.

Brunel's own contentions that wide gauge track was approximately only two and a half percent more expensive to lay may have had an element of truth had it not been for the fact that Brunel himself was the man to lay it – almost literally.

Stephenson's working methods were to delegate the majority of the working activity to competent staff while Brunel, with a much larger ego to contend with, preferred to take a close interest in the most minute detail of every aspect of the work. And it was this near obsession with detail and his inability to delegate which created an impossible workload for himself and of course created huge additional expenses in the laying of the Great Western Railway. Work was completed according to Brunel's specifications and then, upon his personal inspection, found lacking in some small detail, dismantled and started all over again. Contractors asked to tender for work with Brunel would be aware of this tendency toward care and over-attention and therefore put in high tenders against the likelihood of changes and extra work.

Opposite page – "Sultan" with her vast center drive wheel, standing proudly in front of a typical Victorian scene, the Royal Saxon public house in the background.

Bottom left – the result of clearance of a scrapyard in the Azores revealed these last surviving broad gauge engines – seven foot, Brunel gauge, built at Falcon of Loughborough and Black Hawthorn's Gateshead works around 1883-88. The engines were refurbished and are now preserved on the Azores.

Bottom right – it is said that Brunel deliberately built this tunnel at an angle so that on his birthday the sun would shine directly down its entire length.

For the Time Being

The station clock became a feature of all British Railways' stations during the middle of the 19th century when standard time replaced local time and timetables established the necessity to regularize, synchronize and "patronize" the railways of the tiny British islands. Standard time was telegraphed each morning at noon to all station masters who would check their pocket watch and the clock on the platform. Britain would never be the same again.

Opposite page – a picturesque scene gracing the English countryside with far more elegance than the modern overhead motorway.

The standard of work was undoubtedly extremely high and provided the locomotives to be run on Brunel's track every chance of performing at their best. The "Firefly" 2-2-2 class with seven foot driving wheels, established the reputation of the Great Western Railway for speed and economy. On its first run to Bristol the engine reached its destination a full thirty minutes faster than even Brunel had anticipated. This was probably the only time in the history of railways that an engineer's estimates of traveling time were slower than the result!

In Britain "Railway time" was created by the Board of Trade in 1840 and eventually adopted by the entire country as the normal timing system everywhere. Time, according to "Local time" in England was different by several minutes in different areas and the railway timetable system needed consistency to function satisfactorily. It took some while, however, for the railways to run according to any kind of schedule for, engines would break down or run out of water and frequently replacement locomotives had to be called in to keep the system working. But eventually London time was adopted by the railways and transmitted by telegraph each day at noon to all stations who kept their clocks and the pocket watches of the station masters perfectly synchronized thereafter. Trains in England and throughout the rest of the world – except perhaps Japan – have been running late ever since!

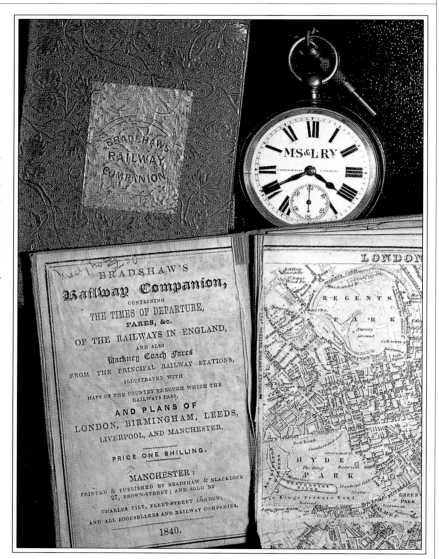

Risky Rails

Left – a typical sign that would instruct travelers on how to use the "communication cord" – very often placed outside the carriage and connected at first with a bell in the engine cab.

Right – France during wartime: soldiers pose in front of a 2-8-0 locomotive.

Opposite page – the engineer's drawings for the general arrangement of the Class "E" 4-4-0 – the English version of the "American."

In 1864 between Bow and Hackney Wick on the North London Railway, a Mr Thomas Briggs was brutally murdered after being robbed and, then tossed out of the train onto the track. The crime was the first of any note to be committed aboard a British steam train. Today, in America or even Britain, such an event may not even hit front page news but in that time it was rare enough anywhere, let alone aboard the supposed safety of a locomotive carriage. Passengers did have a secret fear of violence aboard trains. It was to do with being enclosed in a vehicle that was moving too fast for escape, and women particularly feared the attentions of single men who might, it was fervently imagined, do "anything" within the confines of four moving walls with blinds drawn and doors locked. Worst of all fears, of course, was that engendered by the entry of a train into a dark tunnel. Very often there was no form of light in the early days and a man or woman alone in a carriage in a tunnel was subject to extreme claustrophobia, and often robbery and violence of various descriptions. It was not just a matter of fertile imaginations. Crimes were committed on numerous occasions.

The only answer to this particular problem was of course, the schoolboy's delight – the "pull cord" stop-the-train device, which originally took the form of an alarm and later became a pull cord that connected directly to the engineman's cab, causing the "continuous brakes" to be applied, once they had been invented in the last half of the nineteenth century.

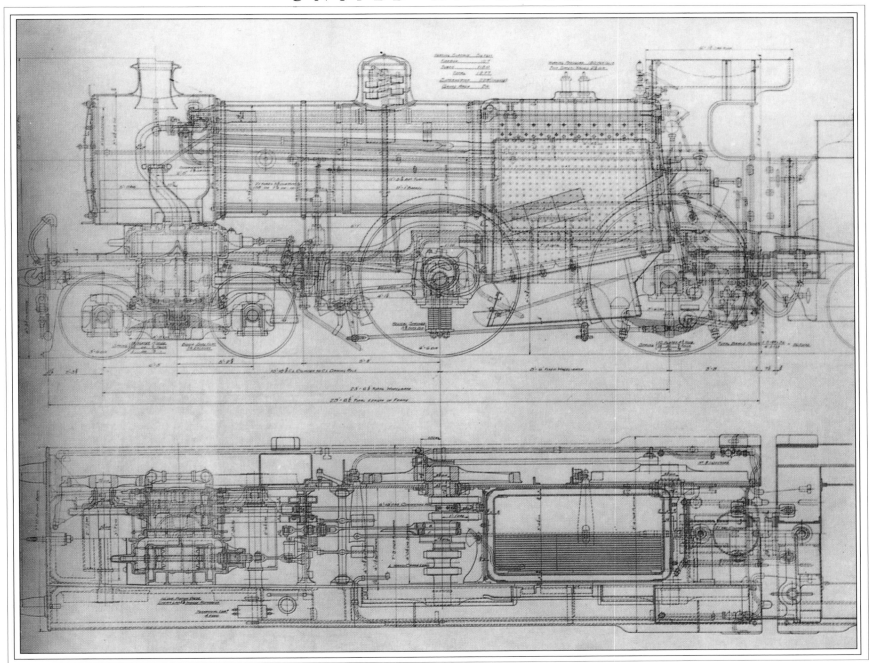

Flying Scot

Opposite page – the early Pullman coaches which were originally imported from America and formed the ultimate in luxury for the express, first-class traveler. The carriages were the first to be heated, with toilets and restaurant cars. On this page is depicted perhaps the world's most famous name plate – the mighty express – "Flying Scotsman."

In any account of steam locomotion there has to be a major spot for the express train and in any account of express trains there has to be the inclusion of Brunel's Great Western Railway, for within that broad gauge system some of the fastest and most glamorous engines pulled some of the most romantic trains anywhere in the world.

In Victorian Britain first-class travel was created for the rich. Suitable decor, safety and comfort were provided. This ethos of comfort and "first-class" has continued throughout rail travel everywhere but applies now more as just an option for those who have the means. As an example of an instance of reverse snobbery within the class structures of the world, Mahatma Gandhi, while in power in India, created no less than four classes of travel on the great Indian railways – fourth for the very poorest people, third for those above the "untouchables" – both "bench" class – second for better off customers, and first class for the very rich; "Air Conditioned" first class is a more recent addition for those who wish to catch colds while in transit! Gandhi himself traveled fourth class but he always took about fifty people with him wherever he went so the fourth class section was therefore invariably taken over by his entourage!

Returning to Brunel and Victorian Britain, the most celebrated engine to take up the banner of express travel was originally the morning mail train in 1848 which took the run from London to Didcot on the Great Western Railway – a journey of fifty-three miles which it was capable of covering in just fifty-six minutes. This was its first stage in the run to the west of England and no standard gauge train could come near to such a record speed. With the authorities of the time lobbying to standardize the GWR track, this sort of performance

was hard to reconcile and the engine that made the trip was named "The Flying Dutchman" after a Derby horse winner of the time. Right up to the 1950s the name was retained and used for the London-to-Plymouth express run and still today excites every train enthusiast.

Express rail travel essentially meant also first class travel – you paid to go there fast, and in first class conditions. For many years facilities were not at all satisfactory and it was only later in the nineteenth century that traveling aboard the trains reached the standard we know today, with the required additional features that we now take for granted. Trains were not heated, lit, divided into smoking and non-smoking carriages and had no toilets. Passengers, after many vehement complaints regarding frozen feet on British winter mornings, finally received offers of foot warmers containing sodium acetate which retained the heat longer than water. Smokers were given their own carriages by law – the opposite of today's drive to limit smoking everywhere – and toilets were finally provided. The British traveler could at last dispose of his legendary self-control!

The most ostentatious example of the raising of standards within first class express travel on the railways in England came in 1874 when the Midland Railway imported the first "Pullman" coaches from America. By British standards they were the most luxurious thing on wheels, with raised roofs for greater light inlet and more space, corridors to allow passengers to stretch their legs and "walk" on journeys and "WC" compartments to walk to. The coaches were well lit with kerosene lamps and properly heated as well as having much better springs in the suspension thus providing more comfortable travel.

Race to the North

The British express train had, by nature, another intrinsic function – speed. Steam locomotion was invented, developed and perfected, fundamentally for one purpose – a purpose which very often overshadowed all other purposes – to get to a destination faster than other means of transport. This determination, especially in the early days, frequently outshone all considerations of comfort and safety, with engineers, railway pioneers and drivers charging along the tracks with a wild abandon as though they hauled nothing but coach-loads of race track enthusiasts. And of course with each successive engine having to be faster than all the others, the competitive nature of mankind shone through like the explosion of a cannon.

One of the greatest examples of this phenomenon in the British Isles was styled "the race to the north" and consisted of the battle to get from London to Scotland on one side of the country faster than from London to Scotland on the other side – east against west.

August 1895 saw the summer tourist traffic to the Highlands of Scotland being the unwitting guinea pigs of the battle between the North Western Railway and the Great Northern Railway. Fashionable travelers would need to follow the style: first, it was only worth taking the trip if Queen Victoria could be seen to be in residence at Balmoral Castle, the royal home in Scotland for the summer; and second, that safely included in the excursion luggage was at least one, probably the latest, "Waverley Novel" by Sir Walter Scott, the "bestseller" novelist

Above – the two bottom pictures show a North Eastern Railway 4-2-2 (top) and the "Hardwicke" 790 (bottom).

Opposite page – the London and North Western Railway "Hardwicke" express engine, one of the legendary locomotives that featured in the "race to the north."

On page 66 – the "City of Wells" running through Kirkby Stephen in 1984 and (page 67) the 777 4-6-0 "Santa Claus" special on the south coast route, Christmas 1984.

of the late nineteenth century. The Waverley novels such as *The Lady of the Lake* or *The Fair Maid of Perth* had an incredible impact on train travelers to Scotland and no right-minded British excursionist could be seen without one.

To get to the tourist resorts of Aboyne, Ballater, Braemar or Banchory, all train travelers – and train was really the only way to get there – had to go via Aberdeen. It was about this time that the mighty Forth Bridge had been completed and effectively shortened the East Coast route by sixteen miles over the West Coast route. Both the east and west journeys were on different track right up to the point at Kinnabar Junction where they converged and had to travel the last thirty-eight miles on the same route. Both routes provided express trains that left London at exactly the same time – 8 PM – from two different stations in London – King's Cross and Euston – with arrival times in Aberdeen of 7.35 AM on the East Coast route and 7.50 AM on the West Coast route – the difference being exactly that created by the difference in the length of the routes. Additionally, according to the timetables of the period, passengers on both trains could alight at Aberdeen in time to catch the 8.05 AM train which would take them on to Ballater, further inland. During the months leading up to this event, the two railway authorities played a game of espionage which would make as good a movie as any in the cinema today. They each posted "scouts" at rival stations to pick up information about changed plans or improvements.

THE CONTINENT

G.W. LMS LNE & SOUTHERN RAILWAYS

Down South

Soot on the Ticket

Collectors today value railway
tickets in the same way as
philatelists their stamp
collections.

Opposite page – a line-up of
motive power at the Leeds
Holbeck toward the end of the
steam age in Britain.

The West Coast special was making the run through all the intermediate stations without waiting for the booked times on the timetables – as soon as the train was ready to leave a station it left and everyone, passengers and all, were expected to cooperate. Once they discovered this the East Coast railway decided to do the same and by August 19th there began an all-out race!

The race became so hot that national newspapers gave it front-page coverage and by the night of August 20/21st the West Coast express arrived at the small Kinnabar Junction in just under a minute before the shorter-routed East Coast train – breaking all previous records and arriving in Aberdeen a full three hours earlier than the booked time, at just before five o'clock in the morning. One can be sure that passengers aboard these trains must have been delighted, having been thrown about, crushed, rolled and shaken for the nine-hour journey, to pitch up covered in soot, fresh as a battered railway "sleeper" at five o'clock in the morning!

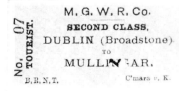

Class Wars

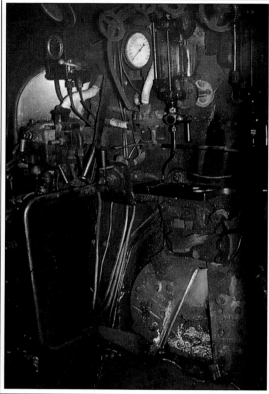

Bottom left – an engine driver in characteristic pose, leaning from the window of a saddle tanker on the Ironstone mines in Northamptonshire, England.

Opposite page – the "Duchess of Hamilton," a modern express with a characteristically royal title.

As a national sport, no doubt, steam locomotive races were fun-and-excitement for those who could afford the excursion, the lack of sleep and the general battering that such an effort would require, but the engineers, the guards, those that operated the engines and tracks must have taken considerable beatings on the long hours of trying to beat the records. It is interesting to note that the locomotives generally had aristocratic names, such as the "Duchess of Hamilton" but were operated by poorly paid, severely overworked, definitely "lower class" men. Such a contrast between the poor conditions of the train workers and the luxurious setting for the aristocrats whose journeys they engineered, typified the social inequalities of the era.

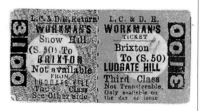

Made in Britain

The last of the English Pacifics
in service in the 1950s. The
dimensions of track, tunnels
and viaducts, laid down by the
mid-nineteenth century created
engines which could not exceed
a certain size. Comparisons can
be shown in the examples from
the other three great steam
nations which developed
without these restrictions.

This engine was one of the
most efficient steam engines
ever created – the superb
French SNCF 4-8-2 P9.

A typical express hauling
locomotive of the Third Reich
in 1936.

A Union Pacific 4-8-4 type
from America.
Above – the three engines that
dominated the 1920s, 30s and
50s.

Small is Beautiful

Britain had always been the country that used the smaller, more compact engine – apart from Brunel's broad gauge systems. This was what the British Isles needed in order to accommodate a smaller country with limited industrial space and no great requirement for massive hauling over difficult gradients or rough track. In effect Britain was always the supreme country for steam locomotion, able to demand the very best machine quality for use on the highest grade railway facilities. Expense had not been spared from the very beginning, as in American steam, and the British railway authorities always afforded best quality work.

While the German giants were being built for German industry and German prestige and the American locomotives were being built bigger and bigger, reaching four and five-hundred-ton weights, the British continued to concentrate on speed and eventually streamlined steam capability right through into the times when the Germans were starting to use diesel electric. But once Germany had brought into use the famous diesel "Flying Hamburger" in 1932 – their first all diesel-electric railcar, able to run the Berlin to Hamburg journey at one hundred and seventy-eight miles per hour – H. N. Gresley of the London and North Eastern Railway invited the makers of this innovative engine to submit their estimates of what such a diesel service could do on the London to Newcastle run. Then, using the engine "Papyrus", he demonstrated that steam – with a four-hour run – could do better. In the course of a single day he broke no less than three world records. Over a distance of twelve point three miles the engine made a speed of one hundred point six miles per hour. Over the three hundred miles round trip the average speed was eighty miles per hour. Even though more precise time keeping methods were now employed for record breaking, such speeds proved the fastest in the world. Based on these figures authority was given for a four-hour service from London to Newcastle in 1935, including a short stop in Darlington – all steam locomotion.

The new train for this run was a two hundred and fifty ton haul, and cruising speeds of ninety miles per hour were planned on level track of a high quality.

Gresley, aiming for the very best, decided to make improvements to the engines that would carry the traffic, and he applied the Chapelon technique of streamlining the internal pipes and through-way systems that we will discuss in the section on France. The new engines were externally streamlined also, and during this year of 1935 – the Silver Jubilee of the British King, George V – the name applied to the train was "The Silver Jubilee." Just to make the final point The Silver Jubilee was finished in silver throughout – locomotives and coaches too.

It must have been an incredible sight to be in London in September of that year and see this glorious train pull into the station for the first time.

Three of the great "little" express locomotives of Britain. The early 4-6-0s of the 1920s gave way to the Gresley Pacifics of the 1930s. The final expression of these 4-6-2s in Britain can be seen in the later versions built in the 1940s and the 1950s. The scale, however, remains the same – for in Britain, "small is beautiful".

On page 74 is a London, Midland and Scottish 2-8-0, No. 13809 and on page 75 is another engine of the same company which is a 4-6-0 express No. 5407. Both engines are seen storming Giggleswick Bank in England during the winter and summer of 1983.

On pages 76 and 77 – the Lord Nelson 4-6-0 making heavy going over Moorland Viaduct in 1983 and another 4-6-0 leaving Blea Moor in 1984.

Driven to the Limit

The British, even in 1935, were ardent enthusiasts of their railway network and thoroughly appreciated anything as glamorous and powerful as a "modern" and brand new locomotive. People came to King's Cross station specially to view the new "monster" even if they did not intend to take a trip.

The run itself was even more spectacular than had been expected with a maximum speed of one hundred and twelve and a half miles per hour with higher average speeds than the record already set for this run. Additionally the passenger cars had seating space for one hundred and twenty-two people in the carriage and another seventy-six people in the restaurant car, as against only one hundred and two seats on the Flying Hamburger in Germany.

The main result of this grand achievement was to establish steam locomotion in Britain for a further period, convincing the authorities that diesel was not yet on the immediate horizon. The next step was therefore to improve relationships between the railway authorities' different factions. Competition is what takes man forward but with competition also comes friction and the LNER and LMS lines of Britain's railways were constantly at each other's throats. On January 1st, 1932, Sir Josiah Stamp had appointed a complete outsider, William Stanier, as Chief Mechanical Engineer to revolutionize the motive power fleet by providing standard designs to replace the dozens of older classes inherited from the consituent companies.

Once the new efforts had proved steam's capability the plan continued to reduce the number of older engines that had serviced the country for many years, scrapping many of them and rebuilding the most up-to-date locomotives in order to have fewer engines running longer working hours.

The result was the "Churchward" standard boiler with tapered barrel and a highly specialized version of the "Belpaire" firebox that had been developed in the West Country. There were several thousand older engines extant on the companies' books and it was these that Stanier intended to rebuild, but his main focus was a passenger run from London to Glasgow – straight through non-stop.

Two prototypes were built in the early thirties, "The Princess Royal" and "The Princess Elizabeth" – named after the present Queen of England when she was still a young girl. These engines were the largest and heaviest seen in Britain in use for passenger service and formed the prototypes for engines that began a legendary first continuous run to Glasgow in 1935. The run was not non-stop as had originally been intended but, with turn-around times of three hours at each end, set the latest standards for British passenger railway.

Naturally the competitors on the other side of the country watched as the London, Midland and Scottish made this new run to Glasgow – the London and North Eastern Railway would have to give thought to their trip from London to Edinburgh.

They did not in fact rise to the bait until they found that the LMS were themselves intending to make a new run also to Edinburgh and this of course brought about action. Competition continued and the race to the north carried on right into the beginning of the Second World War with both sides of the railway battle making better and better speeds with higher and higher quality trains until the outbreak of war brought the whole race to an abrupt halt.

Dying Breed

On page 78 and 79 – once steam locomotion had reached the pinnacle of design and speed, the engines took on a flavor of streamline that would never be bettered anywhere in the world. The LNER "Mallard" attained a speed record of 120 MPH.

On these pages can be seen the contrast to the pinnacle of beauty and design. British steam waned into disuse, the engines slowly disappearing as Doctor Beeching began to shut down vast areas of British Railways.

Inevitably the steam locomotive in Britain had to die. After the best part of a century and a half it had completed its task and run the full course of its development from being a strange little beast with uncertain beginnings to one of the most streamlined and beautiful "boilers on wheels" ever to be perfected by man. When analyzed, the steam locomotive with all its power to elicit emotion was just a large metal container which heated water from a fire, the resultant vapor being used to drive wheels – a most unsophisticated body.

Man's facility to elaborate on such a basic theme seemed endlessly complex at the time and one hundred and fifty years of improving and refining such simplicity bears witness both to our engineering ingenuity and perhaps our preoccupation with trivia. Maybe today we are doing exactly the same thing with modern, infinitely more "sophisticated" technology – such as the airplane – which in one century or so to come will look equally simplistic. Perhaps that's what it's all about – jumping from one trivial pursuit to another!

However there can be little doubt, whether you are a steam enthusiast or simply an innocent bystander, that the whole era of steam traction was a magnificent one. The beauty and excitement of the designs that emerged from steam trains have never been paralleled, and even today amongst the futuristic imaginations of the movie world the whole era is still being echoed. For example in the sets designed and built for the movie *Dune*, in which space vehicles travel the entire breadth of the universe in no time, and resemble something out of the Great Western Railway's engineering yards, steam is regarded as a matter for the expansive imaginations of science fiction writers and buffs.

Diesel electric railway may be more efficient, less costly, faster, certainly cleaner and less elaborate and therefore easier to maintain, but stand in any

station in the world and take a look at it! There isn't a railway company today who would boast about a diesel electric train or any hauling engine. Once the steam trains had stopped running the length and breadth of England and the rest of the British Isles, people could once again breathe the air without choking, travel through tunnels without being covered with the residue of soot, grow strawberries and runner beans without having to wash off the grime,

A Sense of Loss

The bright and clean railway stations of the steam era were to disappear in large numbers when many British lines were shut down during the government cut backs on railway costs. Many are now occupied by private owners who have converted them into homes.

and stand in Paddington Station without being deafened by the noise. But what was gained for the environment was undoubtedly lost in the magnificence, the sheer force and power, the grandeur and the astonishing sound of a huge engine boiling up like a medieval dragon. And those who were involved in the whole ethos of steam took on a status that has disappeared totally today. The station master of a country town was as important as the priest and the bank manager – his blessing on the commuting or vacationing passengers was as important as his acceptance of their investment in his ironhorses.

The stations themselves were a local pride with fresh flowers growing, tourist posters in the waiting rooms, faulty cisterns that nobody used in the toilets and coal dust on the mahogany window sills, carefully dusted down each morning by the cleaning lady who also looked after the church. The main stations in London were, of course, as magnificent in their architecture as any cathedral and probably more often worshipped in. The contrast be-

tween then and now can very easily be seen on a walk down the Euston Road in London. King's Cross Station has been rebuilt and so has Euston, both looking very much like any modern office block in the city, but St Pancras stands alone as an unrivalled monument to Victorian architecture. Its size and its elaborate design are such a sight that the average tourist, lost in London, might think he was outside a royal palace. No doubt tearing this place down is not worth the effort it would take.

Gone forever now are the local milk trains that delivered the huge churns at five-thirty in the morning, the cattle and sheep trains that took the livestock to market and the late night revellers that missed the last loco the night before, sleeping it off in the warm waiting room until the milk train of the following day.

Many of the stations were simply closed when Doctor Beeching, the British administrator, was assigned to streamlining British Railways in the

Left – a beautifully preserved example of memorabilia in an English country station. The enameled signs which resisted the soot and grime of the age, speak of an epoch that, along with steam, is long gone.

Right – the "Evening Star" was the last main line locomotive to be built in Britain.

1960s. Given the job by a misguided Tory government with vested interests in oil and the motor car, Beeching proceeded to close down a huge percentage of the little uneconomic rural railway lines connecting scattered villages and small towns. Under the banner of increased efficiency, Britain's comprehensive railway network was prevented from ever again forming part of a properly coordinated nation-wide transport system.

People live in old stations now, scattered around the country, with the station signs often still intact and the clear evidence of former railway lines in the flat regions of grassland that seem to go off into the distance, forever straight. Small railways can be found in the most unlikely places – at the bottom of gardens, appearing out of overgrown tunnels, with the last scraps of the stations still lying disused beside the silent track. Steam locomotion has virtually gone forever in the British Isles – only the enthusiasts' and the tourists' revival runs remain. And with its passing, gone too is a style and a feeling that will never be replaced.

Ireland

In the troubled areas of Northern Ireland and the more peaceful Irish Republic – just as in parts of England and Scotland – steam survived until the late 1950s with many charming rural lines with often curious and colorful – and sometimes unpronounceable – names. For many years the engines in use were ancient tanks, not always so well looked after, but still a pleasant sight in that beautiful country.

The Great Northern Railway of Ireland went into liquidation and was nationalized during the 1950s, the steam engines put out to grass and replaced, like everywhere else, with diesel. The range of locomotives in use was wide but tended to be the slower, heavier engines such as the 4-4-0 "Slieve Gullion", a resplendent blue and scarlet locomotive that can still be seen in museums and preserved sidings.

Ireland generally followed Britain in the progress of its railways, only making occasional use of steam for a few years after the British change-over to diesel took place.

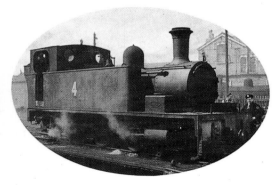

The Emerald Isle

On this spread – Ireland lost her railway systems to the liquidator in the 1950s and nationalization took over the running. Scenes like these would never be seen again.

There were few sights more stirring for the railway enthusiast than the beautiful blue and scarlet livery of the Great Northern Line.

When the Emerald meets the Orange
And steam gives way to something new,
It'll be the passing of the scarlet
And the dying of the blue.

Irish ballad

Germany

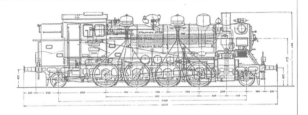

Above – type 86 2-8-2 – one of the last batch of 30 built by Rosen in 1941. The first of these very efficient engines was built in 1928.

European steam traction developed from both American and British influence. It too developed amongst much suspicion! The German people were faced by what their Bavarian College of Physicians called a *delirium furiosum* caused, they indicated, by the excessive speed at which the locomotives traveled. This applied both to those in the trains and those watching them pass.

But delirium or not, the German states within the European developing nations were to produce the biggest and fastest steam traction, equivalent in bulk and capacity to the American vehicles, combining British and American engineering, economics and experience.

"Germany" during the late nineteenth century was still a series of independent states as far as the railways were concerned, and steam development, along with the resulting railway companies, had taken place in each state independently. One of the main contributions made by this part of the world, outside British and American influence, was the process known as the "superheating" of steam. Normally the point at which water boils is dependent on the amount of pressure it is under, so for example if the pressure is two hundred and twenty-five pounds per square inch, the temperature at which water boils and produces steam will be three hundred and ninety-two degrees fahrenheit. However, a Dr Wilhelm Schmidt, working for the Prussian State Railways showed that if steam is further heated –

"superheated" – then its power to work is increased to a much greater extent, as also is its volume through expansion.

Superheaters were therefore fitted to the engines of the Prussian State Railway at great expense, but it was felt that the new efficiency suited the plans of the German people, not only in Prussia but in the other state railways, and also in Belgium, Sweden, Austria, Switzerland and France, where the technique was quickly adopted.

As the German states grew towards the time when a national Germany would be born, each one displayed, at least in terms of railway growth, many of the same characteristics – those of a "grand design" nation with strong outward appearance. This manifested itself in magnificent principal stations which were often designed and built along the lines of palaces. Like Victorian England, where stations like St Pancras and Kings Cross dominated the skyline even more than the churches, Germany worshiped steam travel, even during times of economic stress between the two World Wars, when massive reconstruction of damaged stations took place. The "Iron Chancellor", Bismarck, attempted unsuccessfully to unify German state railways into one system; but the Prussian influence was too great, and in fact these railways tended to decentralize still further during the troubled times before 1914.

Nostalgia in the West

This passion for preserving the grandeur of steam locomotion has continued right through the twentieth century in Germany, as can be seen by the perfectly cleaned and painted museum pieces that now live untouched and unused there. The Germans were in fact one of the very first to make the transition from steam to diesel, with the "Flying Hamburger" of 1932 which replaced steam simply through its unprecedented speed of travel.

The locomotive series 23 2-6-2 was built from 1950 until 1959 as a fast passenger engine – the 23105 was the last of all these engines to be finished by Jung Locomotive Works in 1959.

Working in the East

This rapid progress in the West of Europe away from steam locomotion can be contrasted with the East German "workhorse" which today still functions on the railway lines east of the Berlin Wall. Here we see the evidence of the great "Teutonic" force in action rather than in preservation. East German industry today is still greatly dependent on steam locomotion – note how this difference between the two halves of the country is mirrored in the rest of the world between East and West.

Above – a double-headed goods train hauled by the tiny wheeled series 99, 2-10-2's is seen here as one of the legacies of 1930s Germany.

Opposite – the handsome 2-8-2, No. 41-11180-3, built by Schwartzkopf heads an East German express in 1983.

Ride of the Valkyries

Above – a German giant, of which the blueprint is shown on the opposite page, still in the workshop before receiving her protective skin.

And so came full circle, epitomized in the great "Teutonic fatherland", the wheeled vehicle, running at high speed and making track which moved the produce from field to settlement. Increased speed made for larger centers, greater specialization, greater incentive, greater aggression, more suspicion, more insecurity. In the words of Marshall McLuhan — *So it is that the wheeled vehicle makes its appearance at once as a war chariot, just as the urban center, created by the wheel, make its appearance as an aggressive stronghold. No further motivation than the compounding and consolidation of specialist skills by acceleration of the wheel is needed to explain the mounting degree of human creativity and destructiveness."* (from *Understanding Media*, 1964)

And thus the steam locomotive was brought round from its original coal-carrying workhorse state through the stylish transport of people, back to the workhorse of the industrial and poorer nations of the east of Europe where finance is not available for the improvement of transportation of raw materials.

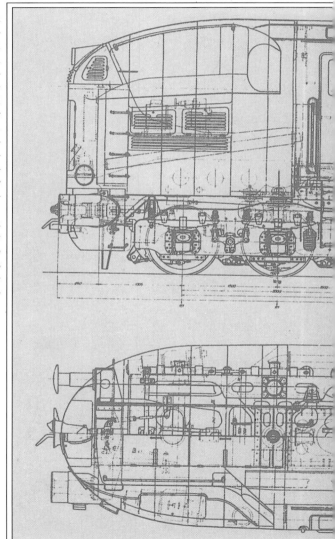

Right – the kind of engineer's drawing that would be the "blueprint" for beginning work on a classic, high-powered engine.

In the late 1930s, the USA and Britain experimented with streamlined, futuristic engines. The Third Reich, having a highly competitive image to maintain, created a series of similar streamline designs which looked more like their diesel counterparts than steam engines. Maintenance crews did not like these designs as they proved difficult when internal work was needed.

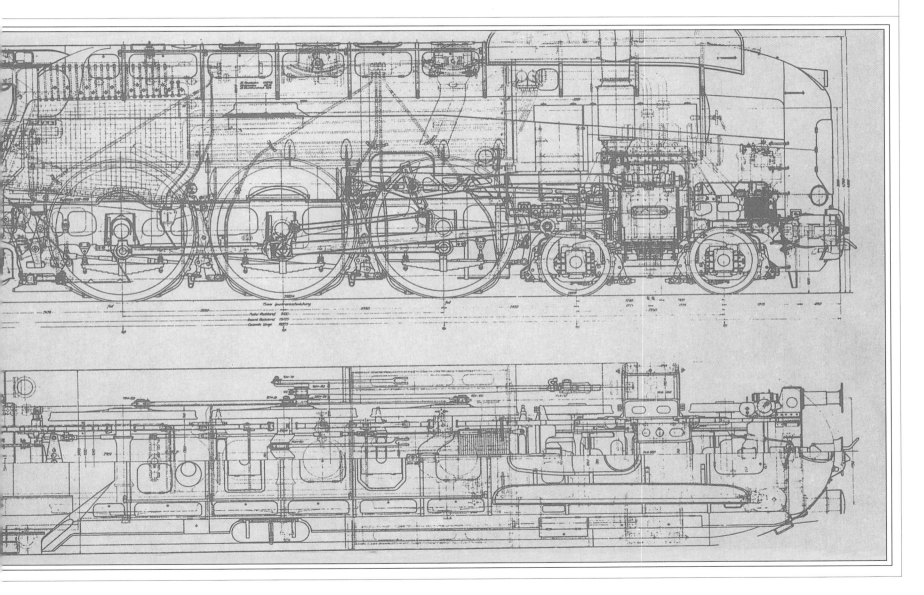

Scandinavia

The challenges involved in steam locomotion were as much in the conquering of the terrain as in the development of the engines. In long distance travel the engine needed power and sustaining capacity – power to cover distance and haul heavy loads and power to climb. But as even the best locomotive will only ever cope with restricted inclines, the steam locomotive needed some help when it came to dealing with railways through the Alps of Europe and then the mountains of Scandinavia, with impractical gradients all the way. One way was tunnels, another the zigzag track and the third double-headers, or engines in tandem.

The Mont Cenis tunnel between France and Italy was successfully completed in 1871 – eight and a half miles of rock – and shortly after, the route from Germany through Switzerland into Italy ran through the celebrated St Gotthard pass – just under nine and a half miles. Prior to this extraordinary accomplishment, the coaches and mail carts had made the hazardous journey over the mountains.

Using a surveying system called "indirect triangulation" the tunnels were bored simultaneously from either end and geometrically linked up between the lines of entry. Bearings were taken over the pass from the approaching valleys and the result was a meeting point of both bores in the middle of the mountain with a deviation of only a few inches.

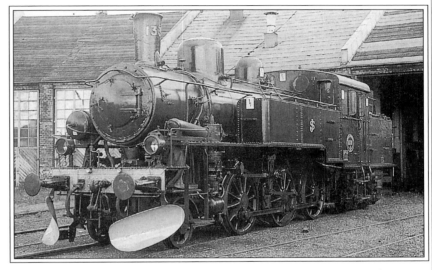

The Scandinavian countries encountered the problems of forest fires from their steam engine sparks. The sheer size of the mountainous areas made any major tunneling impracticable. The very nature of the wild terrain forced the railways down into the valleys. These examples show the sturdy simple engines which would survive the heavy snow-bound conditions of life near the Arctic Circle.

Northern Lights in the Arctic Circle

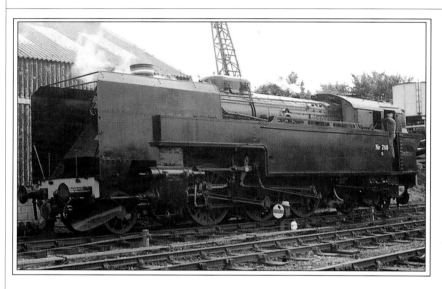

Once into Scandinavia, however, the mountains were just too big and too diverse to tunnel so the railways went around them. One of the biggest problems faced by railway pioneers in the north of Europe was forest fires, caused by the sparks flying from the chimneys, and locomotives were eventually fitted with spark-arresting devices.

But even though the railway systems in countries such as Norway didn't have to deal with massive tunnels, they did have to undergo the most hazardous conditions when dealing with the permanent snow-lines. The most famous of the Norwegian State Railways – the Norske Statsbaner – started work on track at the beginning of this century to connect Bergen with Oslo, the newly-founded capital of a country that had only just achieved independence. Norway had been united with Denmark from the fourteenth century until 1814, and with Sweden from 1814 to 1905 when independence was granted. Norway developed a national consciousness towards the end of the nineteenth century, growing in its industrial capabilities and especially in the field of the arts. Heinrich Ibsen, Grieg and Munch, all emerged into world recognition during this same period of Norway's history, creating a strong sense of the country's worth and enabling the government to achieve separation from Swedish influence.

Above left – a 2-6-2 tanker with a unique streamline and the distinctive red and white smoke stack rings of Denmark.

Above right – taken over the Arctic Circle during a blizzard on the border of Finland and Lapland this picture depicts engine 1074 of the TR1 class on a footplate journey.

The Iron Troll

Steam locomotives were ready right at this time, imported from Britain and America, to run the same line that today still carries tourists from the North Sea through to Oslo. The work took ten years of incredible hardship, with the workforce completely cut off in the mountains throughout the months of winter. Once complete, the journey lasted eleven hours and fifty minutes and when the train reached Voss it faced a climb from sea level to over four thousand feet at Finse. No single locomotive was capable of the incline and a second huge 4-8-0 was attached to pull the load.

And so it was possible to board "The Norseman" in London and travel up the East Coast main line to the Quayside of the Tyne Commission at the mouth of the River Tyne near Newcastle. Here the traveler would undergo the incredible, long journey through dockland sidings to draw up alongside one of the Bergen Line ships. The journey across the North Sea may have been, and sometimes still is, disturbing to the stomach, but at the beginning of the twentieth century the trip was the very first to connect Central Europe to the Arctic regions, north of Scandinavia, completing another link in the iron chain.

Above left – a woodburning class TK3 2-8-0 working the Finnish Railways in 1972 – known as the "little jumbo" by the Finns, they were built for lightly laid track with a rail weight of fifty pounds per yard.

Above right – taken over the Arctic Circle during a blizzard on the border of Finland and Lapland this picture depicts engine 10974 of the TR1 class on a footplate journey.

Austria · Hungary

Inheritors of the Titans

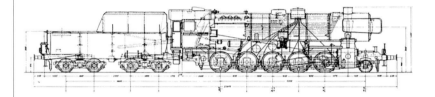

Top right – this picture was taken in Linz, Austria in 1972 of 4-6-2 tanks, the old Austrian Sudbhan Railway, 629 class for suburban service. These engines were reclassed as 77 by the occupying Germans in the Second World War. At the far end of the picture in the back of the shed is a Kriegslokomotive, the German giant so popular all over Europe after the war.

Traveling south again from the snow-covered mountains of the north, the Austrians were preparing to cross the Alps by train some sixty years before the Norwegians tackled the snowy mountain ranges. The Austrian Empire, then including Trieste, felt a commercial and strategic need to open up communications between the Baltic and the Adriatic Seas. What lay between them was the Semmering Range, a part of the Alps that almost defied all the engineering capabilities of man.

Taking inspiration from the American skill in conquering difficult terrain, Dr Karl Ritter von Ghega, in 1842, returned from a trip to the States confident that Austria could overcome the problems it faced. His main study had been the American success in surmounting the Alleghenies, and after long delay in the Austrian arrangements to begin the work, Ghega's route was accepted in 1848.

To give an idea of how incredibly forceful was man's determination during this era of transport growth, it is worth detailing the task that faced the conquerers of the Semmering Range. The proposed track was to be driven through dense forest on the edge of precipitous mountainside. In order to reduce the gradients to a maximum of one in forty, the engineers planned to use "reverse curvature" – a method of traversing steep gradients by zigzagging up

Austro-Hungarian Steam empire

the slopes alternating at each bend between forward and reverse by first running onto a terminal siding. Even so there was a thirty-six mile stretch between Gloggnitz and Murzzuschlag which contained no less than fifteen tunnels, sixteen viaducts and one hundred culverts. In addition it was necessary to erect huge lengths of stone wall to retain the rock falls.

The workforce employed to complete this extraordinary task was drawn from immigrant Germans, Czechs and Italians, and although the engineering and construction work on the track was completed to perhaps the highest standard of any railroad in the world, the labor force suffered the most appalling death and accident toll. No fewer than seven hundred men died during the six years it took to complete the effort. It is easy sometimes to relate the creation of railway lines to that of warfare; as always, the desire of man to advance gives little consideration to life.

Through the immortal renown of Ghega, the problem of the Alpine railway and future similar construction works was solved; the high mountains were opened up at one stroke, after a quarter of a century, to Stephenson's steam railway, and the realization of later Alpine railways was no longer a technical but an economic question.

When the Austro-Hungarian Empire was split up after the World War I, engines were inherited by the resulting countries. This spread the Empire's designs over many emergent lands.

Poland

Keeping up the Tradition

The Iron Curtain hides, sometimes quite effectively, the still living and running Ironhorse. For industrial use, the steam locomotive remains one of the forces still regularly visible and at work in Poland and East Germany. The camera, of course, is not always welcome in many areas of this part of Europe – sadly – as the examples of steam engines continue to proliferate, partly due to the readily available coal fuel.

Above left – an engine plate from the Polish builder Chrzanow – one of the most prolific engine builders in Poland.

Bottom left – a PT 47 class running on a cross country express from Opole to Klodzko. These PT 47 Mikados are one of Europe's most exciting steam survivors.

Yugoslavia

Right – a Yugoslav Railway 51 class 2-6-2T on the Karlovac to Sisak line where she shunts between passenger duties. The passenger coaches were left for the thirty minutes needed to complete the shunting – passengers and all!

On page 110, top left – the Belgrade Locomotive sheds in the early 1970s showing their Vulcan Liberation engines, out of use.

On page 110 – the bottom left engine plate is from Yugoslav Railway's 20 class 2-6-0 number 099 indicating that the engine was built in Düsseldorf in 1922.

On page 110, right – a scene on the scrap-line at Sarajevo and the remains of a 97 class 0-6-4 in front of a condemned 83 class 0-8-2.

On page 111 – a snow scene on the border of Rumania in 1980 with an engine built before the First World War which is still hauling mixed trains.

In some of the countries, such as Hungary, steam locomotion has almost been withdrawn, soon to be completely replaced, as in the West, by diesel traction. But the quality and appearance of existing engines such as the 4-8-0s at work on the very long push-and-pull trains, were until recently unsurpassed elsewhere.

In Yugoslavia steam is almost extinct from the main line, though a very few still exist. Diesels, though, are near to replacing everything. In the

Tito's Titans

Bygone Slavs

Skirts on the Stacks

Left – two engines from
European history, the left
engine being one of Hitler's
war engines – a
Kriegslokomotive – JZ 33 class
2-10-0 and on the right a 28
class 0-10-0s, both freight
engines.

main the locomotives of the Eastern Bloc countries are all painted black – shining black, but black nevertheless. It seems the desire is to condemn them to their task of work. But as an exception to this, the remaining the locomotives in Bulgaria charge across the country in green livery, with red frames and golden wings on the smoke boxes.

And it is here, in the heart of Eastern Europe, that we find some of the most dramatic graveyards of steam locomotion. In Vakarel, for example, a huge death knell has sounded for withdrawn locomotive types, including examples of the massive 2-12-4Ts lying alongside elephantine 15M class 4-10-0s. Sometimes these steam graveyards are still more dramatic and breathtaking than the working locomotives themselves and within the world of steam, the graveyard has certainly remained "alive" for far longer than any motor vehicle scrapyard could manage. This may, of course, have a lot to do with the practicalities and the expense of shifting two-hundred-ton masses of metal, but there is also the business of spare parts. There are few companies left willing or able to manufacture a one-hundred and forty square foot superheater!

The one exception to the decline of steam in Europe is Poland where many classes are engaged in a broad variety duties in different parts of the country. The work ranges from express passenger haulage through to heavy freight and other intermediate duties.

Opposite page – a river scene
in Slovenia with a classic
Yugoslav Railway class 25 2-8-0
silhouetted against the morning
sun.

France

An American designed 141 R, commonly known as the "Liberation," hauling an almost empty goods train. The single car on the train is an evocative reminder of why the railway's dominance as the prime transport system in Europe came to an end with the invention of the internal combustion engine and the super highway.

The Ironhorse was one of the major contributors to the rise of national pride and probably had a lot to do with the First World War. In this respect the steam locomotive brought upon itself both the benefits and the suffering that existed in Europe during the early 1900s. This was so in France particularly, where the mighty compound engine 4-6-4s, created by M. de Glehn – one of the most celebrated of the French engineers – hit the assembly line in 1911. These locomotives were by far the largest and most powerful in Europe at the time, but needed considerable development work and so were abandoned until after the First World War.

By the early 1920s, France, along with other European nations, was in need of considerable rehabilitation within the railway networks and it was only then that the mightiest of locomotives again saw production. The slump years that followed the "Great War" were a time for building up the sagging coal industries, and any change that meant importing fuel was discouraged. Diesel was therefore far from the minds of the French and the English and the steam locomotive stayed alive perhaps for this very reason.

This particular state of affairs, together with a serious lack of funds, brought steam locomotion forward another step in the capable hands of one André Chapelon, who took over the management of the Paris-Orléans Railway in the early 1930s and set about the task of satisfying the need for increased capacity without any funds. In laying bare the inner workings of the large-wheeled Orléans Pacifics, Chapelon found that the high pressure cylinders were generating a far higher output than the lower pressure cylinders. For example, pulling a three hundred and seventy-five ton train at sixty-six miles per hour, the high pressure cylinders produced nine hundred and eighteen horsepower, while the low pressure produced only fifty-nine horsepower – a considerable difference.

This could, in fact, have been one of the first steps towards the final realization that steam, even in its greatest growth period, could never equal the efficiency and output of diesel. Chapelon, however, spent what little funds he was alloted in replacing the cylinders and valves, together with the super-heaters, with more efficient equipment. He added twin-orifice blast-pipes and chimneys, and stream-

Two Schools of Thought

The big 4-8-2 compound had two reverse and forward gears and the engine driver needed to be a fully qualified engineer to drive the locomotive – a massively complex machine.

lined the passages and ports to give the steam a freer run through the engine. As always with steam, the whole package required to make the engine "go" was very simple and only ever required clearing out so that the steam could flow freely to the areas that needed its force. The result in this case, was a thoroughly French appearance with many appurtenances attached to the outside of the engine, but the efficiency of the drive and power was enormously improved with a new three thousand horsepower capacity as against a maximum of one thousand one hundred before the improvements. Not satisfied

Final State of the Art

In contrast to the compound (opposite) the Americans built the 141R (this page) as simple as could be. Called the "Liberation" and delivered to France after World War II to augment the SNCF's depleted fleets, they were, ironically, the last locomotives to run in this great steam nation.

even with this, Chapelon took another engine, an even older one – the 1907 small-wheeled Pacific – and applied the same technique there, also rebuilding the engine into a 4-8-0. The result was still more impressive with a horsepower yield of four thousand.

The results of Chapelon's work were published all over the world and created something of a sensation. By 1931 his methods has been applied in both Britain and America to give way to some of the highest speed records in the history of steam locomotion.

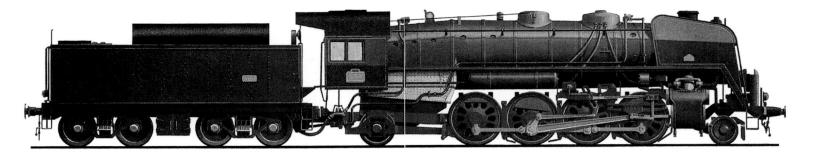

Switzerland

In the later stages of World War I, Switzerland was a very significant country in terms of steam locomotion, but from a point of view that might not seem quite so obvious. As a neutral country surrounded by warring nations, it was used extensively for prisoner exchanges, largely in the town of Constance, a German enclave within the Swiss borders. Taking a steam train which passed through or visited Constance was a hazardous affair — especially if passengers got off the train. Stories are told of Englishmen simply descending for a few moments to stretch their legs or relieve themselves, and immediately getting arrested and imprisoned for the remainder of the war!

A Brienz-Rothorn steam engine, built for mountain climbing work like a Swiss watch.

Built like Swiss Watches

The St Gotthard tunnel, one of the world's most difficult railway tunneling operations, had enemies at either end of it during World War I. To add to the hazards, the incline required double-header engines — two locomotives together — to haul the trains through, and the drivers ran the risk of asphyxiation!

Switzerland was always famous for its beautiful and scenic railway routes and in 1913 one of the most startling of its kind was opened between Bern and Lötschberg on the Simplon Railway, right through the heart of the Alps. The line traveled south from Spiez around the lake of Thun and directly through

On the Brienz-Rothorn Bahn engine motion section for engine No. 7.

Portugal

The Inquisition and Satan's Beast

Portugal once boasted the cleanest and most highly polished fleet of black steam engines in Europe. This lovely "Satan's Beast" seems to confront the very church itself, a testimony to how much has changed since clerics denounced the new sciences as the work of the devil, 150 years ago.

the Bernese Oberland, linking up to the Rhône Valley with the main line Swiss Federal Railways in Brigue at the north end of the Simplon tunnel – one of the longest and most dramatic of the Alpine mountain tunnels. The saddest thing though, for steam lovers, was that this line was electric from the outset! Never was there to be the sight of steam bursting from a locomotive through these glorious routes across some of the most magnificent mountains in the world. The Swiss were concerned with efficiency but also the health of their engine drivers and became one of the very first countries to turn to electric rail.

In a world of mass communications, super highways, airlines and satellite link-ups we tend to forget that it was only a hundred and fifty years ago that man had virtually no means of either fast or sure

travel. Few roads were even passable and anything bulky took months to transport whether by canal or by slow, horse-drawn carts. Man was actually discouraged from moving around.

In that age of small national states constantly at war with one another the cultural shock of the railway precipitated many cataclysmic changes. Europe entered a social and political turmoil exactly at the same time as the steam locomotive made it possible to stoke such a revolution. The railway opened

up opportunities for industrial expansion which had not been feasible before and allowed almost anyone easy access to new places of work or pleasure. More significantly, the military saw the railway as a strategic means of transporting troups, supplies and weapons to any front.

However, those whose vested interests lay in maintaining the status quo were threatened by the new revolutionary machine and resisted the change. The church, finding itself embattled against the whole new development of science, condemned the steam train, alongside Darwin, as "Satan's Beast." Both Spain and Portugal, plunged in economic and political upheaval, raised many voices against the new locomotive, proclaiming it to be a perfect example of "wicked science." Still, the interest of commerce prevailed and the flexing of new national pride soon overrode such issues.

Spain

Iron Bull

Left – a magnificent, green-liveried 4-8-4 working on Spanish Railways – the epitome of the very best and most powerful of Spanish steam – oil-burners that were kept in great condition until the early 70s when they were reduced to secondary work.

Right – a scene from Salamanca of a "RENFE" 240 class 4-8-0 which belonged to the Madrid Zaragoza & Alicante Railway, built between 1920 and 1931 for Spain.

On page 128 – a 19th century German-built goods engine in northwestern Spain which has been pensioned off from the national railways to colliery ownership.

It was only a few years ago that Portugal was still one of the last great meccas of steam pilgrimage in Europe. Portuguese railways had a fine tradition for what was probably the most dutifully clean and polished locomotives in service outside of museums. During an economic crisis in the 1970s, Portugal gave a new lease of life to the remaining sturdy little engines, and they were still operating between the small rural towns and villages on the narrow, meter gauge tracks until recently, when they were consigned to occasional tourist revival runs. While the main broad gauge lines have long since been modernized, it was still possible until not long ago to find 0-4-4-0 Mallets on a Miranda branch line, or 2-4-6-0 tankers on the Corgo line from Ragna to Chaves. But now even there, steam traction is sadly extinct.

The Land of Dante

Italy

Creator of a Nation

Staying in the south of Europe, we go back almost a century to the early days of steam in what is now called Italy. Until 1861 there was no unified Italy but a series of territories dominated in the north by the Austrian Empire – Lombardy. Sardinia also had a foothold on the mainland and in the south stood the Papal States, as well as the Kingdom of Sicily. It was in the south that the first railway was projected, to be laid along the Bay of Naples, planned to start work in 1839. With various extensions and additions the line – the first in "Italy" – eventually traveled from Naples to Capua by 1844. In the north a line known as the Lombard Venetian Railway was built from Milan to Venice. But political unrest – a fond harbinger of steam railway – slowed progress, and the track was not ready to carry the iron monster until 1846. The first known locomotive to thunder across the burgeoning Italian frontiers was a Stephenson 2-2-2 of the "Patentee" type.

A strange thing about Italy and one which is still visible today, is this nation's facility for creating an appearance of chaos which somehow shadows a remarkable design for living and expanding.

A perfect example of this is the way in which various foreign railway companies entered into a vast program of development of Italy's rail in the mid-nineteenth century. Although initial enthusiasm gave way to hard practicalities and it was found that both manpower and finances were exhausted, the national network still managed to extend from three thousand, one hundred and seventy miles in 1865 to twice that figure in twenty years. It was largely state intervention in the form of concessions and guarantees which led to the creation of two main extending networks divided by the Appenines. These railways were the Mediterranean line based in Florence and the Adriatic line with its center in Turin. There was also a very beautiful network in Sicily.

The Appennine mountains had created an almost insurmountable obstacle to communications between the two lines and it took engineers eight years to tunnel and bridge a route. However some of the gradients were so steep that they proved too great for existing Italian locomotives, and a French engineer, Germain Sommeiller, created a unique twin back-to-back engine to solve the problem. With one of the pair running in reverse, these powerful twins worked the line for many years, until heavier and even more powerful engines became available.

As long ago as 1905, Italian railways embarked on a locomotive standardization scheme which laid down the basic concepts for Italian steam traction for the remainder of its existence.

By the 1930s some of Italy's broad gauge lines had been converted to diesel electric, but steam survived well into the 1970s, especially on a vast network of secondary lines, with an interesting variety of locomotive classes based on the standard designs of 1905. Apart from the standby service it remained the last Italian steam traction in operation.

Greece

There is a phenomenon within the cult of the steam locomotive that is unique and will not be found in the same form anywhere else in the world – the locomotive graveyard.

In the world of the motor vehicle, planned obsolescence, poor design and shoddy workmanship have contributed to the car a bad enough name that the "scrapyard" – note the difference between the meanings of scrapyard and graveyard – is valueless. Nobody bothers to take pictures of metal heaps of automobiles. Computers represent the very modern social aspect of technological easy come, easy go. Even ships are usually consigned to the deep or abandoned in disused river beds.

There is barely one form, short of life itself, that warrants as much care as the steam locomotive graveyard. It is even surprising that the mighty graveyards in, for example, Greece, do not contain commemorative stones and small bunches of flowers.

Above – a scene from the Salonica dump showing three British-built, war department, "Austerity" 2-10-0s. These engines were used directly for war efforts in Northern France and England – one hundred and fifty were built in the mid-1940s.

Opposite page – a famous McArthur engine built as American aid to post-war Europe. On the viaduct above the line of war engines is a modern express diesel train, passing the now dead locomotives in line.

Terminal Point

Above – a scene on the Peloponnese peninsula in southern Greece on the meter gauge network. This is a "Z" class 2-6-0 tank which remained in service until the 1970s.

The pictures on the right and opposite page both derive from the same graveyard site at Thessalonica in Greece. In 1986 the dump was cut up and scrapped but in the meantime we can see on the right foreground of the opposite page a 2-10-0 from Austria, built specially for Greece in 1927 for passenger work. Next to this are two 0-10-0s – Austrian 80.9s, heavy freight haulers.

The steam locomotive graveyard has been a tribute to history – a history which contains a supreme effort, a uniqueness of hand-built, man-made determination, never again to be equalled in the future. One major reason why the graveyards grew up is simply that which derives from the sheer size and weight of the engines. It was until recently very difficult and uneconomic to shift two hundred tons of metal, and the result was natural stockpiling. In some parts of the world such as South America in the jungles, engines lie amidst growing foliage which will one day obscure their presence as effectively as the ocean deeps obscured the Titanic. In other areas, such as Pirgos in Greece, locomotives like the "Z" class engines built in France around 1899 lay where they were left to rust, strangely tangled and brown, for years the remaining evidence of an era that burned out through the advancement of the world. Sadly, most of these Greek graveyards have effectively disappeared, cut up and been disposed of at auctions to be sent either for preservation or the foundry.

Steam enthusiasts have a dream of a time when perhaps war will bring a resurgence of interest in steam. There seems to be a complex formula for the rebirth of steam locomotion that works like this: a country that is not highly advanced economically and still contains steam graveyards finds itself in danger of war with a neighboring country. The only and most accessible form of heavy transport that is available is the steam engine and so the remains of graveyards are plundered and locomotives are rebuilt to carry the soldiers and weapons required to fight the war. This scenario almost occurred recently in Greek history during the Turkish-Greek clash over Cyprus.

Colossi of Maroussi

Turkey

The Middle East still provides a fascinating variety of steam locomotives to this day, and Turkey forms a perfect example of this phenomenon in action. In the European sector steam is barely evident but beyond the Bosphorus it still exists. For steam buffs the poor economic conditions have their benefits for, as always, where there are economic restrictions, steam engines prevail.

Unlike a lot of Eastern Europe, the Turks have little problem with the camera and tend towards a friendly approach to enthusiasts. If there is a benefit therefore in the pleasures of recording steam for the future, Turkey and parts of the Middle East are good places to do it.

The main centers lie in Irmak, Izmir, Karabük and Zonguldak. Travelers should also visit Sivas, Kars, Afyon and Adana – all places with suitable local flavor and functioning steam trains.

The biggest influence on Turkish steam railway was Germany – especially the Third Reich and prior to that Imperial Germany. In fact, the Teutonic influence is still very strong, apart from the very Turkish name fittings. By British standards the engines are very large, but the majority of Turkish hauling requires massive pulling power, and the engines supplied by the British during their aid program to Turkey as result of World War II took the form of the LMS class 8F 2-8-0s, odd examples of which survive today.

On these and following pages, Turkish steam thrives in industrial areas of steel production, the engines derived from Germany and America, mostly heavy-weight and powerful and sometimes originally intended for passenger work.

On page 145 – a German Kriegslokomotive – 2-10-0 "war engine" – six thousand of which were built on a basic design for wartime efforts of the German army. Capable of very heavy service in difficult times and after the war passed on to various other countries, including Russia. This example is on the Turkish State Railways.

Warhorses on the Plains

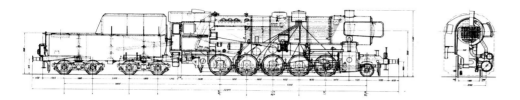

On page 146, left – a pair of American built "Skyliner" 2-10-0s at the depot at Irmak before departing on a double-headed freight train.

On page 146 – the right-hand engine, a veteran ex-Prussian design G82 class 2-8-0, disappearing in its own vapors at Eregli on the Black Sea in Turkey.

On page 147 – at the Karabuk steel works in Northern Turkey waste fills the slag banks.

On this spread – the German desert campaigns revealed engines that would eventually come to work the Turkish industries – powerful, hardy locomotives like the Kriegslokomotive that saw battle and troop movement and needed to withstand tremendously hard beatings.

The Turks inherited the 8 Fs because that design played a special part in the Second World War – the Turks called them "Churchills", engines that were often specially adapted to the needs of battle, the transport of troops and the supply of weapons. The German army relied heavily on the "Kriegslocomotive" because of its power and strength and some of these engines traveled through the worst war conditions and took immense punishment as they brought more soldiers to the battlefront. Their design was so reliable that no less than six thousand of them were built around the time of World War II, and many can still be seen in the industrial parts of Turkey.

Certainly no diesel locomotive would ever have survived the demands made upon these engines, even with the bullet proofing that was provided. Some of them were even mounted with machine guns and the odd turret still exist today.

A few large steam designs found in the world today function along the Black Sea coast where certain collieries also make intensive use of small industrial steam engines. Among the Mosques at Izmir it is also possible to catch a rare sight even now of one of the twenty-seven German 2-10-2s built in the early 1930s as it rounds the steep inclines pulling passenger carriages on the commuter line from the city.

Both America and Britain brought steam to the Middle East, the US providing eighty-eight "Skyliner" 2-10-0s shortly after the Second World War. The British supplied 0-8-0 tanks from Bagnalls of Stafford in 1937 which are used at the steel works originally opened by Ataturk himself.

These engines carry the steel foundry waste to the huge slag banks where it is poured like boiling oil down the slopes – the heat being felt two hundred yards away.

Acknowledgments

The Publishers would like to acknowledge the following photographers, agencies and institutions for the right to reproduce their photographs and illustrations in this book:

K & B News:
Agenzia D-Day / *Pages* – 86, 87, 88, 89, 90, 91, 94, 95, 100, 101, 102, 103, 104, 105, 106, 107, 109, 130, 131, 132, 133, 134, 135, 136, 137, 142, 143, 144, 145, 148, 149, 150, 151

Archivio Fotografico Enciclopedico (Paul Ronald): *Pages* – 2, 3, 7, 11, 13, 111, and endpapers.

Association of American Railroads: *Pages* – 17, 24, 33.

B & O Railway Museum: *Page* – 23.

Bachman, Ellis R: *Pages* – 32, 37.

Bledsoe Rail Slides Series: *Pages* – 34, 35, 36, 37, 42, 70.
Burman, Shirley: *Pages* – 22, 23, 26, 30, 31, 39, 42.

Canadian Pacific Corporate Archives: *Page* – 44.

Garratt, Colin: *Pages* – 18-21, 49-57, 68-71, 80, 81, 99, 106, 108, 110, 112, 113, 122, 126, 127, 138-141, 146, 147.

Marsh, J.C.: *Page* – 78.

National Railway Museum, London: *Pages* – 60, 61, 66.

Paramount Pictures: *Page* – 25.

Pennsylvania Railroads: *Page* – 28.

Santa Fé Railway: *Page* – 28.

Southern Pacific Company: *Pages* – 16, 28.

Winkley, J.: *Pages* – 36, 43, 46, 47, 58, 59, 62-67, 74, 79, 82, 83, 96-98, 115-125, 128, 129.

Union Pacific Railways, Museum Collection: *Pages* – 26, 28.

United States Envelope Company, Paper Cup Division: *Page* – 29.